Praise for *They Ask, You Answer*

"I'm a marketing agency owner and read a lot of books about marketing and sales. *They Ask, You Answer* is the best thing I've read on the topics of content and inbound marketing. I've bought over 60 copies of this book over the past few months and have been sending them to clients and prospective customers simply because no one has done a better job than Marcus at explaining content and inbound marketing in a way that the average person can grasp. [*They Ask, You Answer*] should be required reading for any modern CMO, marketing director, or VP of sales."

—Joe Sullivan, Founder, Gorilla 76

"I just wanted to pass along a huge thank you. I just finished reading your book *They Ask, You Answer,* and it has left me as inspired as I was 12 years ago when I started my company. I read it in less than a day, brainstormed our first 80 topics, and also wrote our first 1,400-word piece on top five problems the same day. This is such a great way to be seen as experts in our field and I can't believe we didn't think of it. We do a great job showing our expertise over the phone, but most people don't call. This WILL change their impression of us without a phone call. Thank you again; you have no idea how much this means for our company, my employees, and their families."

—Greg Knighton, Owner, Beyond the Office Door

"I rarely get 'ga-ga' over an author or a specific book (though I love to read and have my favorite authors). But after finishing *They Ask, You Answer* over the weekend, I felt compelled to connect with you. I started thinking about what impact this information could have on my own business and how I can bring it to other small businesses. As of right now, I typically offer straight-up copywriting and writing coaching to clients. But I just spent 90 minutes with my business coach, hashing out how I can pull your principles into what I do with clients. (She bought your book, too, on my recommendation. We were literally paging through the book to gather ideas and insight during our call.)"

—Abby M. Herman, Write Solutions

"I love that you put the reader into the right frame of mind, almost immediately. I love that you establish the baseline of what it takes to be great. I love that you have the stats that reinforce the message. And I love your ability as a storyteller and your desire to include your own personal examples as well as other related examples. In short: I love it."

—David Moreland, Professor, Lawrence Kinlin School of Business

"I've finished your book yesterday. Brilliant read, and thank you very much. But what a pain! It has changed my perception on things, so today I am working on my own company already, taking your advice on board."

—Lukas Brzozowski, Solobirch

"*They Ask, You Answer* is now my bible in developing an updated strategy game plan for my agency."

—Matt Jacoby, Octave Media

"*They Ask, You Answer* offers the most polished presentation of Marcus' philosophy and processes. It's also one of the most transparent content marketing books I've read. Marcus doesn't hold anything back in [*They Ask, You Answer*]. He candidly discusses pricing and disclosure strategies, qualifying prospects, handling disruptive competitors, and involving his sales staff in the content creation process. It is as close as you can get to sitting next to Marcus in first class and chatting on a coast-to-coast flight. It brought back all of lessons I had learned in retail...the basics that most businesses neglect. (And that most big agencies can't comprehend.) As a lover of carefully written, savvy, helpful nonfiction, I just wanted to share my respect for the freshness and relevance of your book."

—Roger C. Parker

"I came across *They Ask, You Answer* and [have] been able to massively increase the value I offer my customers. I've had a few big projects this year, and in every case, I've advocated a They Ask, You Answer approach to content marketing. I've managed to sell education centers to a number of big B2B clients, and they're all thrilled with the results they're seeing. My reputation as a content writer has sky-rocketed, I'm getting far more business via word of mouth, and my clients are doing better in terms of their customer care and their organic SEO results. I'm able to walk into introductory meetings confidently now, knowing I have a tried and tested content marketing strategy to sell. So, thank you."

–Lorrie Hartshorn, Freelance Copywriter

"Excellent book and sound advice that goes beyond the content marketing buzzword and focuses on providing value-first advice for people who are doing their pre-purchase research. I especially appreciated the strategies shared for getting the Sales team involved in what it typically viewed as 'marketing's job.' The author lays out a great process for winning them over and getting them actively producing content of value to the company's prospects and customers."

–Don the Idea Guy

"This is a beautiful perspective. Rather than the typical 'pump out more content' advice I read every day, this book is all about helping customers. It gives you one of those 'duh' moments where you say, 'If I am producing educational content that answers questions from customers, it will attract people to our company because we're genuinely serving them.' This book centers on the idea that education and helping is the place your content should come from. It's refreshing after reading so many books that focus on vanity metrics like number of likes and shares. There are lots of great case studies in the book, even for companies who are in seemingly commodity-based spaces."

–Lisa Cummings

"This book teaches you core, fundamental, commonly overlooked truths that set the foundation for any marketing campaign you decide to do. You will no longer see marketing as a complex or gamblers' game of attracting sales through any and all means until one way 'just works' to stick to. Incredibly calming and peaceful experience for hardened marketers that have tried a lot of ways to market their products, but are still open to learning and understanding that there could be more that they haven't figured out. Exhilarating experience."

–Doug Mitchell

"The single greatest public speaker I've ever had the pleasure of hearing, Marcus has unmatched energy and passion for content marketing (not to mention SUCCESS!), and he brings all of it to this book. It's practical, easy to digest, and will leave you excited to walk into work the next day and begin fundamental change. I bought copies for my whole team!"

—Dan Gingiss, Vice President, Persado

"Marcus Sheridan knocks it out of the park with the most motivating, tactical, and informative book on content marketing out there. He has changed my business and many others that I know by his simple principle They Ask, You Answer. Such a simple concept that many forget...and Marcus really breaks down EVERYTHING you need to know in order to be successful at this."

—Bella Vasta, Speaker, Business Owner

"Marcus Sheridan shares a formula for success that I've personally witnessed many times as the foundation for today's top performing companies. His simple formula, They Ask, You Answer, ensures that your organization becomes the best teacher on the planet in your field. Marcus shares remarkable stories, brilliant insight, and actionable steps to put your company ahead of the competition. No book can compare to seeing Marcus speak in person, but this is a close second. You'll love this book."

—Ian Altman, Speaker

"This book is The Bible of content marketing and inbound sales. It offers an incredibly powerful yet simple message. It is 100 percent aligned with how customers think—yes, the ones who vote with their wallets and ultimately decide the fate of a business. More than just a book, this is a culmination of five years of testing and proving in the real world. It is for those business owners and marketers who would be willing to temporarily clear away their pre-conceived notions of what they think works, and be open to seeing how a fresh approach has already created transformational success for so many others. I also appreciate how easy it is to read. There's no jargon or filler. Love it!"

—John Soh

THEY
ASK
YOU
ANSWER

MARCUS SHERIDAN

Foreword by Krista Kotrla

THEY
ASK
YOU
ANSWER

REVISED AND UPDATED

A REVOLUTIONARY APPROACH TO
INBOUND SALES,
CONTENT MARKETING,
AND TODAY'S DIGITAL CONSUMER

WILEY

Published by John Wiley & Sons, Inc., Hoboken, New Jersey.

First edition published by John Wiley & Sons, Inc., in 2017.

Published simultaneously in Canada.

For general information on our other products and services or for technical support, please contact our Customer Care Department within the United States at (800) 762–2974, outside the United States at (317) 572–3993 or fax (317) 572–4002.

Wiley publishes in a variety of print and electronic formats and by print-on-demand. Some material included with standard print versions of this book may not be included in e-books or in print-on-demand. If this book refers to media such as a CD or DVD that is not included in the version you purchased, you may download this material at http://booksupport.wiley.com. For more information about Wiley products, visit www.wiley.com.

Library of Congress Cataloging-in-Publication Data:

ISBN 9781119610144 (Hardcover)

ISBN 9781119611004 (ePDF)

ISBN 9781119611028 (ePub)

Cover image: © Alex Belomlinsky/Getty Images, Inc.
Cover design: Wiley

Printed in the United States of America

SKY10031374_111121

Contents

Foreword

"I'm just a construction worker, but when I had a plan and we were working together, we could build a skyscraper. Now you're master builders, just imagine what could happen if you did that. You could save the universe."
　　　　　　　　　　　　—Emmet Brickowoski, *The Lego Movie*

Back in 2010, I discovered something surprising. It turns out that it's possible for an average person to save a struggling business and inspire a major culture change throughout an organization. This book is about how.

How is that possible if you're not the CEO? How do you do it if you work remotely, like more than 1,000 miles away from headquarters?

What if you are the youngest person on the management team? And a female just returning from maternity leave? Do you have to mandate it or is it possible to inspire that sort of change?

How does an average person cut budgets, bring in more sales, shorten the buying cycle, increase profits, get other people to market for you, improve employee engagement, and dramatically grow the business with a simple four-word strategy?

Impossible, you say. *Or is it?*

What if I told you that it is very possible because that's exactly what happened?

Let me share with you a little bit about my journey.

The truth is I couldn't have accomplished any of those things without the help of the ideas, stories, and strategies shared throughout this book, with Marcus Sheridan as my guide.

Here's how it began...

It started with an urgent problem—sales were down. *Way* down. So much so that the company was shrinking. Budgets were dramatically cut, product lines were being abandoned, and team members who were dear friends were let go.

It was devastating.

On top of that, the industry as we knew it was changing and buyers were increasingly more difficult to reach. Emails weren't getting through. Trade shows had half the number of attendees. Mailers weren't bringing in any calls. And don't even get me started on fax blasting—can you even believe there was an era when that worked?

To top it all off, somehow even the smallest of our competitors were showing up higher in online search rankings.

Where had all the buyers gone? How were we going to grow with all this stacked against us?

And who was I to think that I could do anything about it?

At that time, I was the marketing manager at Block Imaging, a B2B that buys, sells, and refurbishes used medical imaging equipment; everything from MRI and CT scanners to digital X-ray equipment. Pretty unique niche, right?

It bothered me that we were a worldwide business and yet only 5 percent of our sales were attributed to online inquiries. This became the single statistic that I set out to change immediately.

This focus led me to discover a concept commonly referred to as "inbound" or "content" marketing. I was quickly convinced that this was the answer to our most urgent problem. So we signed up for the software, and it was going to be a game-changer. Marketing automation and blogging were going to change everything, right?

I was wrong. We needed more than software. We needed information worth sharing. And we needed a lot of it.

So I set out to connect with people in other departments to collect information worth posting and sharing. How hard could that be? As enthusiastic as everyone was, here's the gist of how most of those conversations went:

"Krista, this all sounds very exciting and I cannot wait to see what you do with it. Because I'm in sales, I'm going to go back to selling now. Good luck with your marketing thingy."

New hurdle. **Buy-in.**

I spent the next six months trying to get buy-in and participation. I gave presentations, offered workshops, invited senior sales leaders to attend social selling conferences with me, and unveiled scary statistics as often as I could. Even after all that effort, the best traction I could get was about two blog posts a month. And I was sad.

Sad because I knew the information we were posting was more brand-centric than customer-centric.

Sad because it was taking so much effort to produce sub-par content. Sad because we were running out of time to do this half-assed.

That's when I made the call. It was the call that would change everything.

I needed reinforcements and knew just the person for the challenge.

Marcus Sheridan had been on this exact same journey of saving a struggling small business with inbound marketing. Even better, he had figured out the most simple and compelling strategy imaginable that resulted in millions of dollars in sales: They Ask, You Answer.

His story and examples were just what the Block Imaging team needed to hear. And they needed to hear it from him directly.

It was one of the most important phone calls in my life.

"Marcus, you don't know me or my company yet, but you're my guy. I need you to come help me convince the entire Block Imaging team that going all in with inbound is urgent, important, and that, with their participation, it is going to be the very best thing that ever happened to our business."

As a result of obtaining Marcus's help, we began co-designing a two-day workshop to teach, inspire, and jumpstart a new culture of inbound companywide. Everyone from sales, engineering, leadership, human resources, administration, project management, and general counsel and the entire accounting team were there.

Did it work?

Without a doubt. What I had just spent the entire previous year trying to rally people around, Marcus accomplished companywide in less than six hours.

He simplified the complex.

Everyone understood.

Everyone bought in.

That day marked a new era for our little organization. We now saw ourselves as teachers, and understood that if we just listened well and were willing to answer, things would turn around.

We left that two-day event with 700 blog ideas and inspired content generators in every department.

More important, we had a unified team with a clear plan for writing a better future, both for the organization and for ourselves. Sharing information and empowering buyers became embedded in our culture.

We have since gone from 5 percent of sales attributed to web leads to 40 percent of sales from web leads. In those first two years alone, we could directly tie more than $9 million in sales to inbound website leads.

It feels like we've been given a second chance at life.

We can serve more people in our industry than ever before with less stress. We have more time and energy for our families and friends. We have fun instead of fear and frustration. We have hope instead of helplessness. We are proactive instead of reactive. We have a mission instead of a position.

This is why we are so excited that Marcus is now sharing his wisdom in this book so that others like me may be inspired and equipped to lead this same type of transformation in their own organizations.

Because it is time.

It is time to disrupt the status quo and lead change. It is time to grow an organization that you can be proud of and that buyers trust. It is time to inspire growth in meaningful ways while protecting time and space for the ones you love the most.

It won't be easy, but with this book you will surely push through the challenges faster, and I guarantee it will be worth it.

—Krista Kotrla, CMO, Block Imaging

Introduction

There is a teacher within each of us.

Ever since I can remember, I've believed that statement to be true.

The beauty of teaching is that, at its core, its influence has no bounds.

If I'm being completely honest, when I wrote the first edition of *They Ask, You Answer* and published it without much fanfare and promotion at the beginning of 2017, my hope was it would at least touch a few businesses the way it had touched my life and business years before.

Little did I know it would transform thousands of businesses around the globe. Since its release, the success stories have poured in.

Everything from mom-and-pop businesses to large brands with household names—the impact of *They Ask, You Answer* has been far-reaching and, if I may be so bold, has only scratched the surface of its potential in the marketplace.

Today, the phrase "They Ask, You Answer" has evolved into a business philosophy and corresponding digital roadmap that is now being taught in public universities. But, quite possibly, what has most pleased me is the number of marketers who have contacted me since its release and made such statements as:

"Marcus, finally, my sales team and I are on the same page."

"Marcus, I could never get buy-in from leadership until they read your book."

Considering the prolific problem of internal silos—sales, marketing, leadership—in businesses around the world, anything that could help overcome this issue is a good thing.

I wrote this book with a clear vision of helping leaders and sales teams see digital sales and marketing differently. To help them catch the vision of the "what," "how," and "why" of what had changed, so they could finally get buy-in, gain momentum, and achieve astounding results in an evolving digital world.

With the success of *They Ask, You Answer*, as well as the corresponding feedback from businesses, however, I've realized there were gaps within the first book that needed to be filled. For example, I barely broached the subject of video—and its massive influence on the way people buy—in the first edition.

Also, we didn't answer the question, "How do you create the perfect They Ask, You Answer website?"

(That's something you're going to want to do after reading this book.)

So, in this revised version, not only will we cover these critical subjects, but we will also "look around the turn" at what's coming next. Specifically, we'll discuss what shifts in buyer behavior and technology will be impacting our businesses from a sales and marketing perspective in the years ahead.

Now, just to make sure you have everything you need to make They Ask, You Answer work for your organization, our team at IMPACT—my 60+ person digital sales and marketing agency—has created two comprehensive online resources you'll find incredibly helpful.

An entire They Ask, You Answer resource center. You will find the best examples, tools, and references of just about everything you will read in this book. To find this robust resource center, visit **impactbnd.com /playbooks.**

A powerful They Ask, You Answer scorecard for your organization. By taking a few minutes to fill out this assessment, you will receive a numerical "score" that tells you exactly where you currently stand at your company on following the principles of They Ask, You Answer. Additionally, you will be given a series of actionable recommendations that will point you in the right direction as an organization. To find your scorecard, visit **impactbnd.com/scorecard.**

Finally, I'm going to do something here that may not be scalable, but it's important to me:

My personal email is **marcus@marcussheridan.com.**

I invite you to email at any time with your thoughts, feelings, and questions about the book.

I'm here to help and, as long as I'm not speaking from a stage or spending a moment with my wife and four kids, I'll respond as quickly as possible.

PART

I

A Very Different Way of Looking at Business, Marketing, and Trust

How would you respond if I asked you, "Who is the most trusted voice in your industry?"

Surprisingly, in most industries, such a person or company doesn't even exist. In the following pages, if you truly apply what is taught herein, you'll discover exactly how you can become that voice.

1 | The Fall

I could feel the anxiety and sense of hopelessness start to overcome me. Like every night at this time, driving home from a long day of work, I dialed my phone and waited for the bank's automated system to tell me what our company's checking account balance was.

With heart racing, the response was not surprising.

Overdrawn.

Why was I even checking at this point? Our company bank account had been overdrawn for the past two weeks.

For some reason, though, I still dialed that stupid number and held out a faint hope that we were in a better situation than what reality demonstrated.

After hanging up the phone and feeling the weight of the world on my shoulders, I started to cry.

I was 31 years old. My business was a failure. My family life was suffering. And for a guy who sees himself as a problem-solver, I was out of answers.

So the tears kept flowing.

I knew that, when I arrived home in a few minutes, my wife, Nikki, would likely not even ask me the standard question, "So how was work today?"

You see, some questions in life are better off not being asked. My wife understood that. She'd gotten used to seeing the strain in my eyes and the worry in my countenance. The pain was self-evident.

Such was the life of a pool guy in January 2009 . . .

How I Became a "Pool Guy"

Upon graduating from West Virginia University in 2001, my plan was simple: get an interview and get a job.

By this point in my life, I was already married and had my first child, Danielle (eventually, we'd have four children).

Initially, my plan worked out. I identified a company that I thought would be a great fit, got an interview, and was offered the job immediately. Nikki and I loaded our daughter in the car seat, along with the few belongings we owned in a U-Haul, and headed off to live near Washington, D.C., as I would work in the northern Virginia town of Vienna.

Unfortunately, it didn't take long for me to realize I wasn't thrilled about my new job. To make matters worse, my wife hated Washington, D.C., traffic. So before we entrenched ourselves too deeply, we left the area and headed back to the area where we grew up—the "Northern Neck" of Virginia—in order to regroup and figure out what our next step would be.

It was during this time that two of my good friends, Jim Spiess and Jason Hughes, had just started a swimming pool company—River Pools and Spas—and were in the process of opening a small retail store (selling hot tubs, swimming pool supplies, and so on) in the quaint town of Warsaw, Virginia.

Knowing they needed someone to run the retail location while they installed above-ground and in-ground swimming pools for customers, Jim and Jason asked me if I'd consider managing the store.

My response should give you a good feel for where my mind was at the time: "Sure, I'm happy to help you guys get going until I find out where I'll be working next."

It's a statement that makes me chuckle to this day.

You see, no one ever says, "I want to be a pool guy when I grow up."

I certainly never saw myself with this title when I was younger, or when I graduated from college. But life is a funny thing.

As soon as I started at River Pools, I quickly realized I didn't know much about the industry. Simply "knowing how to swim" wasn't going to help me sell hot tubs, pool chemicals, and the like.

So I did what I always do—I learned. I read. I studied. I dug deep into the industry. I didn't know how long I was going to be a pool guy, but I did know I didn't want to look dumb in front of customers.

Before long, I started to know a lot about pools and spas. In fact, when Jim and Jason would come into the store, I would quiz them on hot tub brands, distinguishing features, key components, and other subjects. It didn't take them long to realize I suddenly knew a lot about the stuff we sold. Customers, too, could see that, if they had a question, I generally had an answer. And if I didn't have it, it would bother me so much that I'd assuredly study it so as to better respond on the next occasion.

It was for this reason that Jim and Jason believed I would be the ideal third partner in the business, asking me at the six-month mark whether I would join their team for good.

Having no idea the impact this invitation would have on my life, I simply responded, "Yes."

That was the year 2001.

2001 to 2008: The False Economy

Growing a business is never an easy thing to do. It doesn't matter the field, or the industry, or the area—it isn't easy.

Nor was it easy in the early years of River Pools and Spas.

There were victories, and there were defeats.

There were many good days and many bad ones as well.

But one thing is for sure—the economy of the United States during these years (specifically, the housing market) made it so anyone in the home improvement industry could grow a business and make a decent living, even if they weren't particularly good at what they did.

For River Pools and Spas, the strong economy meant that home values were bloating to ridiculous levels, which therefore enabled almost anyone (if you had a heartbeat, you qualified) to get a second mortgage or a home equity line.

In other words, for the first seven and a half years of the 2000s, anyone could get a loan for a swimming pool.

If you (the pool guy) could sell it, they (the homeowners) would find someone to give them the money for it.

Looking back, it doesn't speak too highly of our country's economic system, but it was what it was. And everyone was a part of it, present party included.

2008: The Wheels Start to Fall Off

The year 2008 started off with so much promise. Our company had been through more than our share of ups and downs, and I was invigorated with the prospect of having a banner year.

Finally, it looked like we were going to turn the corner and generate sufficient revenue to go into the offseason with enough savings in the bank. (In Virginia, the main sales season for swimming pool companies is March to September.)

By mid-summer of that year, sales were higher than they'd ever been. I can remember looking at the calendar thinking, "Wow, we have two months' worth of pools sold that need to be installed—this is amazing!"

But then, like a sudden earthquake that no one is prepared for, in September of that year, our country's economic system collapsed.

Lehman Brothers went belly up.

The Dow crashed.

John McCain and Barack Obama were on the campaign trail debating what should be done with the failing banks.

It was a chain reaction that seemed to grow worse and worse every day.

In fact, within 48 hours of the Dow's crash, we at River Pools and Spas had five customers who had put down deposits to have a pool installed during the winter months essentially tell us, "We're too worried about the economy and cannot move forward with our swimming pool project."

With the average pool installation cost being in the $50,000 range, this equated to roughly $250,000 in losses, all within 48 hours.

To say it was a huge blow would be an understatement.

Over the coming months, things went from bad to worse. Our savings, and then our credit, were completely depleted.

By December 2008, we had to tell our employees to stay at home because there was no work to be done.

By January 2009, our business checking account was overdrawn.

Things got so bad that my business partners and I met with multiple business consultants, only to be told, for all intents and purposes, that it was the end of the road for River Pools and Spas

It was time to file bankruptcy.

This pill was a difficult one to swallow. We had given that little swimming pool company everything we had over the previous eight years, and now we were going to not only lose it, but also our homes, our credit, and our foreseeable financial future.

And so there I was, crying in my car that late night in January 2009—account overdrawn, employees sitting at home, and staring bankruptcy square in the face.

No doubt, it was a dark and difficult time in my life.

2

A Massive Buying Shift and the Blur Between Sales and Marketing

Before we move on with the fall and, ultimately, the rise of River Pools and Spas, it's critical we address a couple of fundamental truths that, unless understood and embraced, will prevent you from getting anything out of this book whatsoever.

The first is this: *Consumer buying patterns have gone through a monumental shift over the past decade.*

Specifically, the line between "sales" and "marketing" has been completely blurred, if not totally erased.

Multiple recent studies have shown one specific eye-popping statistic: *Today, on average, 70 percent of the buying decision is made **before** a prospect talks to the company.*

Yep, 70 percent.

In other words, before the sales pro ever enters the fray, 70 percent of the buying decision has already been made by the consumer.

And if you're thinking this is a business-to-consumer study (B2C), you're wrong. In fact, originally, this was a business-to-business (B2B) study.

Simply put, the 70 percent number resonates across the board regardless of business type, size, location, and so on.

Let's take a minute to analyze what this all means.

If we went back a decade or so and asked what percentage of the buying decision was made before someone actually talked to the company, what do you think the number would have been?

Most folks would estimate between 20 and 40 percent, as would I.

So if we go with this number and were at 20 to 40 percent a decade ago, yet find ourselves at 70 percent today, what's the number going to be during the next decade?

Eighty percent?

Ninety percent?

One hundred percent?

Furthermore, let's swallow an even greater pill, one that is weighing on businesses and brands all over the globe:

If this shift is true, which department of your organization has a greater impact on the actual sale? Is it the sales department or the marketing department?

Yep, marketing.

But, generally speaking, when a company is in financial trouble, which is the first department that gets laid off?

Once again, marketing.

And when a company is looking to grow the business, which is the first to be hired?

Sales.

So the question is: *Why are we doing it this way?*

Because, as I'm sure you'd agree, we've been doing it this way for well over 100 years.

Sales, in the past, was always viewed as the revenue driver.

Marketing was the expense.

But no longer are we able to say this.

And no longer can businesses and brands continue to do things the way they've always been done. In fact, as we are thrust into the digital age, it's the ones who aren't doing business as it has always been done who are experiencing the greatest success.

Again and again, as we look around the marketplace, businesses and brands are breaking the rules and defying industry norms to create new rules of doing business.

Zappos did this when they said consumers could ship their shoes back at no cost. At the time, their competitors scoffed. Today, they're all following suit.

Zappos changed the rules.

CarMax, a company we discuss later in this book, revolutionized the used car industry.

How did they do it? As you'll learn, they simply listened to what consumers wanted ... and acted on it, regardless of whether those in their industry thought it possible or not.

Again, CarMax changed the rules.

The list of examples could go on and on, but the commonality across these companies would remain the same. They clearly understood consumers had changed, and they knew they had to react or get left behind.

The simple fact is, sales and marketing will never be the same, and the line between them will only become more and more blurred over time.

And anything that you and I think must be sold face-to-face will eventually be sold online.

Scary?

Yeah, I guess you could see it that way. Or you could see it as a major opportunity, just as so many businesses have done while experiencing extraordinary results.

Case in point, just last year, my swimming pool company sold multiple swimming pools that were more than $100,000 ... *before* we ever set foot in the customer's homes.

Had you told me this was possible just five years ago, I would have laughed in your face.

Today, I realize I was naïve.

In fact, I'm not sure any of us fathom just how much consumerism and buyer patterns are going to change in the coming years.

But this much I know:

If you adhere to what you read in the following pages, you'll at least be prepared for what comes next, whatever that may be.

3

This Book Won't Work for You If...

As mentioned in the previous chapter, two things will dramatically affect whether this book has a positive effect on you and your business.

The first, which we just discussed, is the shift in consumer buying patterns and how it has affected sales and marketing as we know it. If you do not believe there is a change in the way buyers behave, **there really is no reason to continue reading at this point**.

The second element that will affect what you get out of this book is much more personal, and it comes down to a specific mindset.

You see, as I travel the world and speak on the future of sales and marketing—and what businesses must do to be prepared for said future—I find there are two types of people. (And you've likely also seen these types time and time again.)

The first type of person (or business), when they hear a new idea, suggestion, or business strategy, responds with:

"Sure, I can see how that's possible."

"I think we might be able to apply that to our business."

"I could see how that would be used within our industry."

And the second, as you may have guessed, is the opposite of the first.

"Nope. Won't work."

"Couldn't be done."

"That's not how our customers buy in our industry."

And on and on.

For the latter, the reason for such a mindset is simple, and it comes down to one somewhat comical (and sad) belief:

*"But you see, Marcus, the stuff you're talking about here may have worked for you and your swimming pool businesses, but at my company, **we're different**."*

Ah yes, the "We're different" phenomenon.

Funny thing is, I've polled live audiences all over the world, asking thousands of people this one simple question: "How many of you, by a show of hands, believe your business is quite different from the rest of those in the room?"

And what do you think the results of this question are?

If you guessed 100 percent, you're right.

Everyone thinks his or her business is different.

Everyone.

Oddly, no one ever says, *"Actually, Marcus, we're just like that company over there."*

If one looks at the psychology of this response, the reason why 100 percent of people truly believe their businesses are different is because they want to feel *special*.

Whether we want to admit it to ourselves or not, this need to feel special runs deep in the world of business.

But that's the thing. *We're not special.* At least we're not special in the most fundamental sort of the word. Case in point, when I was busy leading the life of a pool guy, my business and sales successes were, ultimately, built on one thing: *consumer (buyer) trust.*

Then, after I moved on from being full-time with River Pools and Spas (to become what is today a silent partner) and started my digital sales and marketing company, which merged with IMPACT (impactbnd.com) in 2018, once again, I found my business and sales successes were built on that same factor: trust.

The fact is, *every* business has a single tie that binds them all together when it comes to consumers and buyers, and that is trust. And the companies that embrace this reality, and let go of the obsession that "we're different" are often the ones doing incredible things in their space.

To further make this point, my digital sales and marketing company, IMPACT, has worked with hundreds of businesses and brands all over the world to help them adjust to today's buyer. More than half of these organizations have been B2B. Many have been serviced-based. But for each one of them, the big picture doesn't change.

We obsess over gaining buyer trust, no matter what title the person has on the other end. In fact, you'll see many of their case studies throughout this book.

This is my challenge to you: This book will certainly, at times, challenge the way you have done business in your space or industry. When this occurs, don't push aside what is being suggested and automatically dismiss its merits. Instead, ask yourself the simple question, *"But is it possible?"*

If you do, I can promise you the information found within these pages will have a dramatic impact on your business—and perhaps even your life.

Whether you're B2B or B2C or a non-profit, local or national, service or product, or whether you're big or small, don't put yourself in the "different" corner.

Bring it back to the basics. Bring it back to trust.

Trust is the business we're all in.

This will never change.

4

The Discovery of They Ask, You Answer

There we were, on the brink of financial ruin.

If we were going to save the company, we needed a miracle, and it had better occur fast. Unless we found a way to garner more leads and sales than we'd ever had—even though there were fewer potential buyers (because of the economy) than ever before—we were going to go out of business within a matter of months.

Despite this crushing weight, I found myself having moments of reflection about the state of business and economics in general. I believed that times were changing. The way people were buying, shopping, and consuming was dramatically different than it had been just a few years before. All I had to do was look in the mirror to see this change.

I was now turning to the internet for *everything*. If I had a question, I went to Google and asked. No longer did I need to be an uninformed consumer for anything. Now I had all the knowledge I needed at my fingertips to become an expert at anything I wanted to master.

If I wanted to find a product or company reviews, tips, tricks, or anything else—it was all there. It was almost as if every consumer was becoming his or her own salesperson or subject matter expert.

They were fascinating times indeed—for me personally, as well. Despite all the stress I was under, I could not stop thinking about the digital opportunities that seemed to be available to any and every business that was willing to notice.

It was clear as day to me that the internet was going to change the world and dominate our lives way beyond what I could even fathom. Over the previous years, I'd sensed this stronger and stronger and stronger. The "old-school" way of advertising wasn't working anymore.

In the past, we had tried everything to generate leads at River Pools—TV, radio, newspaper, the Yellow Pages—you name it. Every year we'd spend hundreds and thousands of dollars to advertise on these media platforms. And every year their efficacy was diminishing exponentially.

Seeing this changing of the guard and knowing things would never go back to the way they were, I knew I had to do something about this problem—and do it quickly.

If my business partners and I were going to save the company, it was time to get our arms around this whole internet thing and discover how it could save River Pools and Spas from bankruptcy.

So I threw myself in.

Every extra minute of the day I had, I started reading about how to leverage the internet to grow our business. As I read articles and watched educational videos (the majority of which I learned on the site HubSpot.com), I noticed certain phrases popping up with great frequency, all of which were quite new to me:

- Inbound marketing
- Content marketing
- Social media marketing
- Digital marketing
- Blogging
- And many others

They were fancy words and terms, and their definitions included a whole lot of marketing-speak that was frankly above this pool guy's head. But, if I may be completely transparent here, I think that's what saved me. I didn't view the internet from an MBA's standpoint. I didn't have years of formal business, sales, or marketing education. Rather, I saw it from a consumer's mindset.

"Inbound marketing," as I understood it, was simply the process of attracting (instead of chasing) customers.

And "content marketing" was simply the act of teaching and problem solving to earn buyer trust.

This basic way of thinking, in hindsight, was a massive advantage.

And to me, as I read all of these fancy words, suggestions, and strategies, it all came back to one core thought:

"Marcus, just answer people's questions."

"OK," I thought, *"I can do that."*

After all, that's really what I am at heart—a teacher.

And so all we had to do as a company was become a teacher of fiberglass swimming pools. Once we came to this realization, our company motto shifted dramatically.

Little did I know that this shift, and the new motto, would go on to affect businesses all over the world.

But it did. And it still does every day.

And as you've likely guessed, the motto was:

They Ask, You Answer.

5 | They Ask, You Answer Defined

What is "They Ask, You Answer"?

More than anything, it's a *business philosophy*.

It's an approach to communication, company culture, and the way we sell as a business.

It starts with an obsession: "What is my customer thinking?"

And when I say "obsession," I really mean that. It extends past "What are they thinking?" to "What are they searching, asking, feeling, and fearing?"

Some companies think they understand these questions, but the fact is most do not.

And having a set of defined "buyer personas"—at least the way many are defined—doesn't count as sufficient either.

When an organization embraces They Ask, You Answer, they believe it's their duty to be the teacher, the go-to source within their particular industry. One that's not afraid to answer any and every question the prospect or customer may have. For them, it's a moral obligation to provide this level of education, regardless of whether the question is perceived as good, bad, or even ugly.

Not only are they willing to address these things better than anyone in their space, but they also allow this to dictate the direction of their business as the future unfolds. Because they are so keenly in tune with what the marketplace is thinking, feeling, and asking, they see where their business model needs to go, evolve, and head toward.

Throughout the remainder of this book, we cover—extensively—this philosophy of They Ask, You Answer.

You're going to not only understand its dramatic impact on River Pools and Spas, but you're also going to witness its impact on multiple companies from various B2C and B2B industries around the world.

You'll also see how this philosophy extends far beyond the scope of "internet marketing" and transcends every element of your business philosophy. From online marketing and face-to-face selling to company branding, this is a way of doing business that could revolutionize everything about your company, your culture, and your bottom line.

In Part 1 of the book, we look at They Ask, You Answer and its impact on your digital marketing efforts. In particular, we focus on how it guides a company's "inbound" or "content" marketing efforts. (For the sake of ease, these words are used interchangeably throughout the rest of this book.)

In Part 2, we discuss how They Ask, You Answer affects the sales side of the business—the way you sell, your sales culture, and the way sales departments are set up in general.

In Part 3, we examine the implementation of this methodology in your business, showing you the *who, what, where, when, why,* and *how* to make it all work.

In Part 4, we take a deep dive into creating a culture of video within your organization and turning video into an essential sales tool going forward.

In Part 5, we show how to create the perfect They Ask, You Answer website. We also look ahead to trends and technology that will be affecting all of us as businesses moving forward.

Finally, in Part 6 of the book, we take some of the commonly asked questions most organizations have upon hearing this approach to business and answer each one to resolve any concerns and fill in any knowledge gaps you may have.

We hope it will be the finishing touch to taking your business and brand—regardless of type, size, or industry—to a place of strength for years and years to come.

6

Brainstorming the Questions You Are Asked Every Day

Now that I'd discovered the core business philosophy we'd be adhering to as we moved forward with River Pools and Spas, it was time to act.

My first action was simple: I sat down at my kitchen table late one night and brainstormed all the questions I'd received about fiberglass swimming pools over the previous nine years.

As you might imagine, the writing was fast and furious. After all, I sold swimming pools for a living. I heard questions from prospects and customers all day long, so the idea of simply recalling these questions was by no means difficult.

After about thirty minutes, I had more than 100 questions listed on the paper.

Wow.

But what happened next is where things became very interesting. I (along with two of my business partners) took those questions and, over the coming months—late at night when everyone in my house was asleep—we wrote articles or made videos answering every single one of them.

Most of these articles were published to our website as blog articles, with the question itself becoming the title of the post. The videos produced were uploaded to YouTube and placed on the website.

For me, this whole process became somewhat of a religion. If I was on a sales appointment, as soon as the prospect would ask me a question my immediate thought was: *"Have I answered that on our website yet?"*

Keep in mind, I'm not talking here about one- or two-sentence answers to questions. I'm talking about *really* answering the question with deep explanations. And we approached each question with a "teacher's" mentality, without bias—our sole obsession was simply one of thoroughly educating the reader.

At the time, I had no idea this little brainstorming activity and corresponding content production would end up being something I'd use to help guide numerous other sales and marketing teams. I never could have imagined that during the coming years so many other businesses around the globe would embrace their own forms of They Ask, You Answer.

The fact is, every industry has hundreds of questions about what prospects and customers want to know when they're making a buying decision. Whether it's B2B or B2C, people want to feel like they've made an informed buying decision, and they certainly don't want to make any mistakes.

The irony is that despite the hundreds of questions that exist in these industries, most company websites don't even address more than a few dozen of these them.

It's a digital paradox of sorts.

As consumers, we expect to be fed *great* information.

As businesses, we like to talk about ourselves and therefore don't focus on what our prospects and customers are thinking about, worrying about, and asking about.

The whole thing is contrary to the very nature of that which we call "building trust."

This brings us to the first major step of They Ask, You Answer.

Putting It into Action

Have a Brainstorming Session

Brainstorm every question you've ever been asked by a prospect or customer. Focus on their fears, issues, concerns, and worries. State them on paper exactly as the buyer would ask (or search) them, not the way you (as the business) would state them.

Once you've completed this list, you have the foundation for your entire digital marketing editorial calendar—be it articles, videos, podcasts, and so on—to put on your company website.

Note: If you struggle coming up with these questions, there's a frank reason why—*you've lost touch with your ideal customer or client.*

If this is the case, it's time to get with your sales team, customer service team, and everyone else, and relearn what your ideal customer wants to know to be able to make an informed buying decision.

7 | The Ostrich Marketing Strategy

Before we dive into They Ask, You Answer, it's important to note another sales and marketing strategy—one you likely weren't taught in business school (but is commonplace around the world today) that is the literal opposite of They Ask, You Answer. I call it "ostrich marketing."

Why is it called ostrich marketing? When an ostrich has a problem, what does it do? It buries its head in the sand. (Yes, it is a myth, but we'll go with it anyway.)

And why does it bury its head in the sand? Because it thinks the problem will go away.

But does the problem ever go away? Of course, the answer is no.

Now, you're probably wondering what an ostrich has to do with you, your business, and the way you communicate online and offline.

Look at it this way—how many times have you been asked a question by a prospect or customer and thought to yourself: *"We'd better not address that issue on our website. Let's just wait until we are talking face-to-face with the prospect and then, if he or she asks about it, we can bring it up."*

My guess is this has happened to you many times. And if you can't think of an example (of the subjects you've ignored), you will. As you read the following pages, you'll find many examples of subjects you have very likely shied away from talking about on your website in the past simply because you *thought* it would put you at a disadvantage, and you wanted to be able to control the conversation.

27

But therein lies the entire problem with ostrich marketing—consumers (just like you and me) don't like it. To put it more bluntly, we abhor it.

Here are the facts about ostrich marketing (or ignoring the questions of your prospects and customers):

- In the digital age, the ostrich does not win.
- The ostrich does not engender trust.
- The ostrich does not get the phone call, the store visit, or the online purchase.
- The ostrich does not get anyone filling out contact forms on his or her website.

The solution? Don't be the ostrich. Do whatever it takes to earn their trust.

Embrace They Ask, You Answer.

8

The CarMax Effect

To truly understand They Ask, You Answer, you must see that it goes well beyond the scope of "Let's produce articles and videos on our website to answer customer questions."

In fact, as previously mentioned, They Ask, You Answer is a *business philosophy*. It's the willingness to be so focused on and obsessed with consumer questions, wants, desires, and needs that you're willing to change and evolve your entire business model around these elements.

To understand this on a deeper level, let's talk about a subject that, without fail, elicits a *unique* emotion from consumers: *buying a used car.*

When you hear the phrase "buy a used car" or "used car salesperson," what is the emotion you experience? What words come to mind?

Sleazy?

Sales-y?

High pressure?

The list goes on and on.

Consumers all over the world share these same negative thoughts. Having spoken to audiences in multiple continents and across different cultures, I can assure you that no one ever shouts, "Trustworthy!" when I ask this question.

This phenomenon begs the question, how did the used car industry get to this point? What happened to make so many consumers around the world lose trust in an entire industry?

To answer this question, let's look at the specifics.

If you were going to go out and buy a used car today, what would be some of your (potential) fears?

29

Across hundreds of global audiences, the answers are almost always the same:

- You don't want to buy a lemon. (You don't want a car with a bunch of problems, false mileage, bad history, and so on.)
- You don't want to have to haggle with the salesperson—the high-pressure sales tactics, back and forth with the sales manager, etc.
- You want to make sure you're getting a good value and not being ripped off.
- You don't want to buy the car and then find out it's the wrong vehicle for you—a.k.a., buyer's remorse.

For years, consumers have had these fears when buying a used car, but few companies cared about addressing them.

That is, until CarMax came along.

The Beginnings of CarMax and a New Way to Sell

The story of CarMax is a powerful one. Based out of Richmond, Virginia, this company went from being doubted by an entire industry of peers to becoming what is today the largest retailer of used vehicles in the United States. Now, you may not think that this fact is profound until you analyze what they did to reach the pinnacle of their industry.

Essentially, CarMax did two things other used car companies weren't willing (at least at the time) to do:

- Admit their industry had a problem (no consumer trust).
- Ask themselves what it would take to earn that trust back.

You see, most businesses and brands never like to admit there is anything wrong with their company, industry, or the way business is generally done. Instead, much like the ostrich, they simply convince themselves it's business as usual—ultimately, ignoring needed change.

But CarMax was the antithesis of the "business as usual" paradigm. Specifically, they did what almost no one else was willing to do.

The first action they took to garner trust back from consumers was to attack the issue of "I don't want to deal with the salesperson" head on by offering what they referred to as "no-haggle pricing." In other words, with no-haggle pricing, consumers were given one listed price for the vehicles, nothing more, nothing less.

For example, if you walk into a CarMax today and write a check for $29,999 on a car that's listed for $30,000—they will not sell you the vehicle unless you come up with another dollar.

Some might argue this hurts CarMax's ability to create urgency and scarcity with the buyer, but the opposite is true. Consumers love the fact they have but one number (price) to focus on, ultimately lowering their anxiety levels while phenomenally boosting trust for the brand in the process.

But CarMax didn't stop there. Beyond offering one price, they also set up their sales team on a flat-rate, one-commission structure—meaning whether they sold the most expensive or the least expensive car on the lot, they would get the same commission.

As you might imagine, by doing this, CarMax has eliminated salespeople's need to think about themselves (wanting a higher commission) over the consumer (finding the right vehicle based on need)—ultimately leading to dramatically more trust during the buying process because customers believe the company, and the salesperson, have their best interest at heart.

Even though competitors originally scorned this sales philosophy at CarMax, the result was groundbreaking, and in the process, CarMax overcame the issue of salesperson distrust—the biggest plague facing their entire industry.

But CarMax continued to take things further. They recognized other fears consumers had and again sought to eliminate them—regardless of the way it had previously been done in the industry.

Their next groundbreaking move came when they started offering a five-day money-back guarantee to customers. In other words, if you bought a car from CarMax and realized during that first week the vehicle was not a good fit for you (for whatever reason), they'd take the car back.

At the time of offering this, the idea of a five-day money-back guarantee was, for most car dealers, preposterous.

In fact, to this day, in many countries the idea is still foreign and unheard of.

But because CarMax was building a consumer-centric business philosophy (that permeated every facet of their company), they simply didn't care whether other companies were or were not offering this type of guarantee.

The end result?

Once again they were able to overcome, and practically eliminate, one of the biggest fears in buying a used car—buyer's remorse.

Another groundbreaking CarMax move was how they turned their attention to quality control. Instead of following the traditional pattern of selling vehicles with previous issues or problems in an effort to net huge profits, they took the necessary steps to ensure they could limit these issues to the best of their ability.

To give you a sense of this, if you walk into a CarMax as a consumer today, one of the first questions they are going to ask you is "Are you familiar with the process by which our vehicles qualify to be sold on our lot?"

Their next action is critical for building trust in that they take the time to physically show you the intensive inspection process their cars have to go through in order to meet their vehicle standards. Furthermore, they *want* you to see how the majority (roughly 66 percent) of the vehicles they buy (in trade-ins or straight from consumers) never make it to the sales lot.

You have likely heard auto dealers brag on their commercials or websites about their "90-point (or thereabouts) inspection process" to ensure vehicle quality. Although CarMax may not have started this trend, they were certainly one of the first to physically *show* each of these inspection points to their potential customers.

After all, seeing is believing.

You see, in business, just talking about something isn't enough. If you truly want to overcome concerns and make your point real, you need to show it. You must teach it. And you certainly must be willing to address it.

In our digital and visual world, one thing is for certain:

If you don't *show* it, it doesn't exist.

Saying "We have great customer service" is likely said by everyone else in your industry. And if everyone is saying it, you can be assured it means nothing to the consumer—that is, until you show it.

The same goes for every other overused business adjective that typically litters business copy, slogans, and website messaging.

CarMax proved this point by physically showing customers their vehicle inspection system. Furthermore, they were one of the first brands to add a CarFax vehicle history report as a standard with all their vehicles—allowing the prospective buyer to see a vehicle's history, once again eliminating seeds of doubt and adding further confidence for the buyer.

As you might imagine, between demonstrating their intensive vehicle inspection process and showing the vehicle history report, CarMax was able to overcome a third major consumer fear: *the fear of buying a lemon.*

At this point, CarMax has now eliminated three major fears of buying a used vehicle:

- Dealing with the salesperson
- Buyer's remorse
- Buying a lemon

As mentioned earlier, there is only one more consumer concern left:

- Not getting ripped off (or wanting to get great value, which is essentially the same thing).

And how did CarMax overcome that fear? Well, the answer is simple. Besides listing the Kelley Blue Book value with all their vehicles, they did the other things you read above.

By taking these steps, CarMax allowed the consumer to sense the extreme value. In this case, it's the value of trust, which is the entire reason for the rise or fall of any brand and business.

But imagine for a second that you went back in time 20 years and were tasked with speaking to a group of 100 used car professionals on how to increase sales and revenue with their businesses. Now imagine telling them that the key to their future success would be found by offering no-haggle pricing, a five-day money-back guarantee, an intensive inspection process with the goal of never selling a lemon again, and a way for consumers to trust in the value of the car.

How do you think that audience would have responded to such recommendations?

Yep, they likely would have thrown you out of the room.

And the reason they would have thrown you out is because such recommendations were practically heresy two decades ago. In fact, there was a time when used car companies laughed at the CarMax business model.

But today, these same companies have now had to change their business models to match that of CarMax's.

You see, every industry is made up of two groups: those who listen to the consumer and act (They Ask, You Answer), and those who maintain the status quo.

But time and time again, history has shown us that those who listen to the consumer and change their business models—regardless of what others may say—set the standard for their space. They become the rule makers.

And the competition? Well, they become the rule followers.

I hope you can clearly see that the amazing story of CarMax can be applied to any industry—regardless of B2B status, B2C status, size, locality, and so on.

In fact, with many of our clients (spread across multiple industries) at my company, IMPACT, we've applied this "CarMax Effect" again and again, often with astounding results.

Simply put, the greatest companies and modern-day rule makers are obsessed with consumer fear, and they allow that fear to dictate their entire business models. They do this because they know that if they are able to eliminate all fears and negative emotions from the buying process, the only emotion left to feel is trust. And trust, quite frankly, is really what this book (and being in business) is all about.

Uber did this in the transportation space by rating drivers and coming up with dramatically more customer-friendly ways of transportation.

Zappos did this in the clothing space by offering free returns.

The examples go on and on, but the principle remains the same.

Consumers ask for it, smart businesses answer it—and often change history in the process.

I'll share one last story about CarMax, one that would be hard to believe if I hadn't been there myself.

In early 2016, I found myself speaking to a company in Houston, Texas, telling them the story of CarMax. When I was done, the owner of the company stood up and stated:

"I agree with everything Marcus has said. In fact, I once bought a car (a Porsche even!) from CarMax but ended up returning it the first week. Why did I return it? Well, my dog didn't like it and couldn't seem to get comfortable, and that's exactly what I told the company when I returned the vehicle. I didn't believe they'd actually refund my money until I saw a check in the mail for the full amount four days later."

I told you the story was crazy.

But such is the stuff legendary companies are made of.

Well done, CarMax.

Putting It into Action

Have a Healthy Relationship with Fear

Allow it to guide your business.

The following activity, albeit incredibly simple, can do wonders for your business, so give it a try. I've done this with multiple organizations to produce profound results.

Just as we did with used cars, take a moment to brainstorm every single reason (fear, worry, question, concern) as to why someone would *not* buy from your company. What would hold them back? What would keep them from clicking "buy," swiping their credit card, or writing that big check?

If you do this activity properly (especially if you do it with fellow employees), you should come up with ten to 20 reasons, if not more (sadly, a surprising number of businesses struggle with this one small task, all because they've lost touch with the most important part of their business: what the potential customer is thinking).

Once you've listed each of these fears or reasons for not buying, now comes the critical step: How many of these issues (fears, worries, concerns, questions, objections, and others) have already been addressed well (a few sentences don't count) on your company website?

How many have been addressed within your sales process?

(Seriously, take the time to do this activity. If you don't, you're going to not only miss the whole point, but you'll also miss a chance to discover some very interesting things about your business.)

If you're like the majority of the brands and businesses I've consulted with, when it comes to your website, the answer is almost always between 10 and 20 percent of the issues.

In other words, the majority of companies never take the time to properly address the biggest fears of their buyers (and leave it to the face-to-face part of the sales process to overcome these objections), and it's costing businesses millions of dollars each year.

So the question is, is it possible for you to address, and even eliminate, all of those issues you wrote down?

Find a way to do this, and you'll likely revolutionize your industry and innovate in ways you previously had not imagined.

But it all starts with an obsession with knowing their objections, and then being willing to do something about them.

This is They Ask, You Answer.

9

The Discovery of The Big 5

Within a couple of months after commencing They Ask, You Answer on the River Pools and Spas website, I could see that what we were doing was already making a difference.

By publishing four to five pieces of content each week on our site, it seemed like searchers (those people looking for swimming pools) and search engines like Google were clearly taking notice.

We were getting more web traffic.

Leads started to increase, many of whom were more educated and qualified because of the content they had read and consumed.

Even a few sales were being made.

Although we weren't breaking the bank, and even though we (and the economy) had a long way to go, there was real progress.

It was exciting.

After about six months of They Ask, You Answer, I took the time to take a deep dive into our web analytics in an effort to pick up on any patterns that may have been occurring. Essentially, I wanted to know what was working, what wasn't working, and the types of content that were getting the most traction and results.

What I discovered was profound.

Basically, there were five types of content subjects (or types of questions) that seemed to move the needle with readers more than anything else, ultimately rendering the greatest amount of traffic, conversions, leads, and sales. These five subjects were as follows:

- Pricing and costs
- Problems
- Versus and comparisons
- Reviews
- Best in class

At the time, I didn't realize that these five subjects weren't at all specific to the swimming pool industry. Rather, these are the five main subjects consumers and businesses research the most whenever they're getting ready to make a purchasing decision.

As mentioned multiple times already, what I'm explaining here is not a B2B or B2C issue. It's all-encompassing, as our studies have shown time and time again.

Once I realized how these five subjects transcend all industries, I dubbed them "The Big 5," and their influence remains as great as it has ever been.

But there is an interesting difference between how businesses and consumers approach The Big 5.

As consumers, we often obsess over these five subjects when considering a purchase.

As businesses, we generally ignore or even hide from these questions, hoping they'll magically go away or, worst case, willing to address them only when we are face-to-face with the prospect or buyer.

In other words, we're experiencing a literal paradox of business strategy, while essentially *not* doing unto others as we would have them do unto us.

Although you may be confused about how to understand and implement The Big 5 in your business, the following chapters cover each individually and show you specific ways you can address these five critical subjects, ultimately winning the trust of searchers and search engines alike.

10 | The Big 5, Topic 1

Pricing and Cost: Why We Must Talk About Money

Have you ever researched online how much something costs?

Assuredly, if you're alive, you have.

But when you're on a company's website, and there is nothing about the costs of their product or services, what is the emotion you experience?

Frustration, right?

I've asked this question to hundreds and hundreds of audiences, and overwhelmingly, "Frustrated" is the number one response, which is exactly why I've dubbed it the "F-word of the internet."

But let's analyze this together for a minute. What gives you the right to be frustrated when you're on a business's website and you can't find any cost or price information?

For starters, you're frustrated because you feel like you're wasting your time and not finding the answers you're looking for.

Furthermore, you're thinking to yourself, *"I'm the customer! It's my money. And it's my right to know."*

But if we look at this at an even deeper level, you're upset because *you* know that the *business* knows the answer to the question. And because *you know* that *they know* the answer, you now feel like they are *hiding* something from you.

When you're researching a company and their products and services, the moment you feel like anyone is hiding anything from you, all trust is lost.

Let's continue, though, to analyze our online behavior in this moment of frustration at not finding the information you're looking for.

Do you say to yourself, *"Well, I'm just going to dig a little deeper on this website and see if I can find the answer?"*

No, of course you don't do that. In fact, the idea of staying on a website that clearly doesn't have what you're looking for is almost insulting to your internet intelligence.

Or do you say to yourself: *"Oh, it's OK that this company is not talking about their prices, I'm sure they're a "value"-based business. I'll just call them instead."*

I bet you don't say that either, do you? In the past you may have called them, but today, you don't. Instead of continuing to dig on their site or calling them directly, today you keep looking. And you do it elsewhere.

And you continue to look until someone answers your original question. Whoever is willing to answer your question first, in most cases, is the one who will get the first phone call or contact. They're also the one who will likely get your business. In other words, they are the one who has earned your trust.

The search behavior just described is consistent for just about any company and culture around the world. As consumers, we expect answers. When we don't get them, we become upset and leave. Our loyalty is to the honest and open teacher focused on *our* problems.

Do you, right now, on your company site, talk a lot about the cost of your products or services? If you are like the thousands of others who've heard me ask this question, you are likely starting to experience a little bit of internal strife contemplating why you do or do not discuss pricing on your website.

There might even a civil war going on inside your head.

I have found that fewer than 10 percent of all businesses in the world (not including ecommerce) address pricing and costs on their company websites. It doesn't matter whether they are B2B or B2C businesses, or whether they are product- or service-oriented, only a small percentage ever address the question of pricing and costs.

The question is, "Why?"

Why are you (assuming you fall in the 90 percent) not currently discussing cost and price on your website?

Regardless of company or culture, we have found there are three reasons businesses justify not discussing this subject on their websites:

- "Every solution is different. Our prices vary."
- "If we discuss pricing on our website, our competitors will find out what we charge."
- "If we show what we charge, we'll scare customers away."

"Every Solution Is Different"

I'm sure this statement is true, but look at it this way: When was the last time you were on a website, couldn't find pricing information, and said to yourself, *"Of course they can't talk about pricing, there are simply too many variables."*

If you're anything like most consumers, you frankly don't care that a company's prices vary. In fact, with any common sense, you already know this. You understand they can't be exact, but you do certainly feel the least they could do is give you a sense for what to expect and some possible ranges as to where you might be.

As a business, you must ask yourself whether it's possible to discuss this question of variable costs. Could you explain the factors that keep the costs down? Could you explain the elements that push the cost of a project up? Could you help the readers (or viewers, listeners, or other type of customer) understand all the factors that dictate cost within your industry as they're doing their research?

Chances are, if you want to give the potential customer a feel for how pricing works within your industry, as well as how pricing works within your company, you could very likely do it.

"Our Competitors Will Find Out What We Charge"

This objection to discussing pricing and cost transparently is often the most laughable. Most companies already know exactly—or at least have a very good feel for—what their competitors charge.

In other words, it's not a big secret.

Everyone knows what everyone else is charging.

It's almost like saying you have a "secret sauce" when, in reality, everyone knows it's just Thousand Island dressing.

Plus, if you consider this even further, you have to ask yourself why you'd ever let the competition dictate your ability to educate, and ultimately gain the trust of, your ideal customers.

One of these groups takes your business, and the other *is* your business.

"We'll Scare Customers Away"

Think about this one for a second. It's as if you're saying, "If I'm honest, people won't want to do business with me."

But if we look at how *we* behave and what *we* expect as consumers, the thing that actually scares us away is the idea of a company *not* addressing cost and price on their website.

To illustrate this point, imagine you're taking a friend to dinner tonight and you all have decided to try a restaurant you've never been to. Before going, if you're like most people, you're going to research two main things before you walk through their front doors—online reviews (via sites like Yelp) and the restaurant's website to look at their menu.

Well, what happens if you go to the menu and you find that it lists items but *not* prices? What do you do?

If you're like most people, you'll decide not to go to that restaurant—not because you couldn't afford to go there, but rather because of the simple fact that they didn't want to show their prices, which planted seeds of doubt in your mind as the consumer. And, as consumers, where there are seeds of doubt, inaction and the inability to make a buying decision almost always occur.

Folks, discussing cost and price is not about affordability, it's about psychology. It's about trust. And believe it or not, every business (yours included) can do it, as we now explain.

11

How One Article About Money Generated More Than $6 Million in Sales

For years in my career as a pool guy, whenever a potential customer would call me, within the first five minutes of a conversation I would almost always hear the same question:

"Marcus, I'm not going to hold you to it, but could you at least give me a feel for how much something like this is going to cost?"

For a long time, that question bothered me as a business owner. I wanted to talk about products, benefits, and features, but the customer wanted to immediately know about pricing.

In hindsight, the fact that I let this bother me so much was foolish. If roles had been reversed, I would have wanted to know the same thing.

In other words, as consumers and buyers, we at least like to have a sense of how much things cost before we spend hours upon hours dedicated to learning about that product, service, company, and so on.

Once I stopped thinking like a business owner and started thinking like the consumer (They Ask, You Answer), I realized one of the most important pieces of content I could produce would be the one that addressed the question, "How much does a fiberglass pool cost?"

So, after years of not wanting to address this subject until I was face-to-face with a prospect, I shifted and wrote the article shown in Figure 11.1 on my company website.

In it, I explain how buying a fiberglass pool was much like buying a car—there were many options, accessories, and so on. I listed each one, offering to the consumer a true sense of the potential scope of a project.

Next, I explained different types of packages we offered as a company: how some buyers wanted a pool in the ground without any patio, landscaping, or other features, and how others were just the opposite—wanting a true "turn-key" installation, complete with patio, fencing, landscaping, and so on.

With each of these, we gave large ranges as to what the buyer might expect to spend, but ultimately, after 1,000+ words of explanation, we said the answer to the question of "How much does it cost?" was "It depends."

Figure 11.1   Fiberglass Pool Cost Article, "A Guide to Fiberglass Pool Costs" by River Pools.

What happened next was very, very interesting.

You see, when I published this article on our website in 2009, take a guess as to how many other swimming pool builders had addressed this question on their company websites?

If you answered zero, you are correct. No one did it. Out of the thousands of pool builders around the globe, every single one of them was the ostrich with its head in the sand.

And, of course, the reasons why they didn't address it were the same reasons we discussed earlier:

- Each project is different and therefore costs vary.
- They didn't want their competitors to see their pricing.
- They were afraid they'd scare prospects away if they honestly discussed pricing.

But for us at River Pools, the fact that no one had addressed this question meant a blue ocean of opportunity for the business. The marketplace was dying for someone to be open and honest enough to address this question, and so that's exactly what we did.

We saw immediate action on two fronts.

Within days of posting the article on our website, we noticed an increase in qualified, productive conversations with leads who contacted us. Many people commented on how impressed they were to "finally" find a company that was willing to discuss the subject of cost and price on their website.

But with search engines like Google, things became even more interesting. Within 48 hours from the time I posted the new page on our site, the article became the first article to pop up any time someone went online and searched anything to do with how much a fiberglass pool cost.

In fact, here is a list of keyword phrases for which this article ranked first in Google search engine results, all within days of publishing the post:

- How much does a fiberglass pool cost?
- How much does it cost to install a pool?
- Cost of in-ground swimming pool

- Fiberglass pool cost
- Fiberglass pool pricing
- And on and on

Now, you might say, *"Well, that's fine, but website traffic doesn't necessarily equate to money. It takes more than traffic to get a customer."*

And if you were thinking this, you're exactly right. What we're discussing here isn't about getting more traffic to your website. Fact is, web traffic doesn't pay your bills, *sales* do.

Luckily, the digital sales and marketing tools we used on our site allowed us to track how people were finding our company and what they were searching for when they found us.

Over the course of time, we saw how this one article would send our company more than one million new visitors, thousands of whom would eventually become leads and hundreds more who would "request a quote"—all because they originally had searched a phrase that had to do with the cost of a fiberglass swimming pool.

But here is the key question: If that article had never been written, would any of those sales appointments have occurred?

The answer, of course, is no.

The prospective buyer (very likely) never would have found us and shown up to our site in the first place—all because we hadn't been willing to address the subject. But in our case, *we were willing to address the question.* And because of this, search engines like Google showed that article (and our website) to thousands and thousands of potential buyers. And because of that, many of these potential buyers were able to say to themselves:

"OK, now I have a much better sense of what would drive the cost of a fiberglass swimming pool up or down. I now know what to expect."

With this education came a feeling of trust, and many visitors eventually filled out a form to get a quote for a swimming pool. Because we're able to track the people who filled out a form (from the cost article) and know which ones bought a swimming pool, we know the value of each one of these customers—a value that can be directly tied to that one article that was written about the cost of a fiberglass pool.

Here is the culminating point: We know that since the time this article was written on our site in 2009, it has made our company more than

$6 million in additional sales—revenue we would *not* have had we been an ostrich with our heads in the sand.

Think about that: *$6 million in sales* simply because we were willing to explain to prospective customers that the cost of a fiberglass swimming pool depends on several factors. Without exaggeration, this single article saved my business. It saved my home. It saved the homes of my two business partners. It also saved the jobs of all our employees.

But the funny thing is, we never specifically stated how much a fiberglass pool costs. We simply answered the question the best we could. We were honest. We openly discussed the industry as a whole. And in the process of doing that, my entire business and, ultimately, my life were altered dramatically.

Fellow reader, this is the power of honesty, transparency, and seeing yourself as a teacher. But sadly, most businesses, especially in the B2B space, still don't recognize this massive need to openly discuss the issue of pricing, budgets, money, and related topics on one's website.

As mentioned earlier, I now have a digital sales and marketing agency, IMPACT, that helps companies all over the world generate more trust, traffic, leads, and sales. More than 50 percent of these clients are B2B. And with more than 80 percent of all of these clients, the number one traffic, lead, and sales-generating content has to do with money, costs, and even salaries. (If you're looking to recruit great people, answer their questions about salary.)

Remember, it doesn't necessarily matter what you specifically say in terms of the numbers. What matters is that you're willing to teach your prospective customers what would drive the cost up or down and help them get a feel for the marketplace.

Over the years, I've had dozens upon dozens of companies approach me and discuss this matter of pricing, only to tell me how they simply can't discuss numbers on their website because their competition charges so much less than they do.

My response is always the same:

"Why is their product or service cheaper?"

Almost always, the response has to do with overseas manufacturers, low quality, customer experience, and so on.

Once again, my retort is always the same:

"Have you bothered to explain these factors well on your company website?"

In almost every industry, consumers make poor buying decisions and purchase the "cheapest" products and services, not because they are solely price motivated, but rather because they don't know any better. They haven't been educated. No one has bothered to truly explain the good, the bad, and the ugly of the industry. And that, once again, is the fault of the business, not the consumer.

Along these same lines, at IMPACT, any time a client of ours states specific pricing on their site, they inevitably find such a strategy generates better, more qualified opportunities.

With specific pricing on their site, they spend less time dealing with prospects who never would have been a good fit in the first place and instead focus their energies on educated, ideal-fit prospects who aren't just looking for the cheapest thing, but rather the best value.

My point to you and your business is this: **When it comes to money, you cannot be the ostrich with your head in the sand.**

You must be willing to address the most important questions— regardless of whether you're service, product, or value driven, and so on. Remember, it doesn't matter what you and I think—what matters is what consumers think, how they behave, and what they expect.

Are you willing to meet their expectations?

Or, would you prefer that the competition be the one who answers the question for them? They're going to get their answers from someone, so wouldn't you prefer they get their answers from you?

Putting It into Action

Focus on Cost, Price, Salary, Etc.

Based on what you have now read, would it possible for you to address the question of pricing and costs (or even salary) on your website?

Remember, I'm not suggesting you put a "price list" on your site. Rather, be willing to specifically address the main pricing questions you get. To do this effectively, complete the following activity:

- List all the major products and services you sell.
- Once this list is complete, identify the items and services that generate the most revenue and/or have the most opportunity for you as a company.
- Now, for each one of these, produce at least one article and video explaining the factors that dictate costs, what the buyer can expect to see in the industry, and where you fall as a company.
- Place this content on your company website. In fact, we strongly recommend to clients that they have a "pricing" tab on the home pages of their websites, and that the content funnel visitors to the articles and videos that address these core pricing questions.
- Immediately start using this content throughout your sales process (as we discuss later in the book).

12

Case Study 1

High-End B2B Technology Company Generates More Than $8 Million in Additional Revenue

Note: As mentioned previously, throughout this book we integrate powerful stories of businesses that have embraced They Ask, You Answer in their own ways to achieve extraordinary results. As is the case with Segue Technologies, you will hear about them embracing strategies that are covered later in the book. When this occurs, you can simply consider it a preview of what is to come in later chapters, as it all will become very clear by the end.

In today's world, few industries are as competitive as technology. In order to stand out in these types of businesses, companies often have to embrace new and creative ways of thinking and doing things, or watch as their businesses slowly fade into oblivion only to be replaced by the next guy who had the foresight to embrace the vision of the future.

Segue Technologies is a perfect example of a company that saw the power of great teaching and transparency as a new and more efficient way of doing business and quickly set out to be the first, and best, to do it in their industry.

51

About Segue Technologies

Segue Technologies specializes in application development and support services for federal, commercial, and nonprofit companies looking to have their IT challenges solved.

Segue provides custom web applications, solves data management problems, and supports the evolution of the mobile workforce. Segue's goal is to help clients customize their IT services in a way that saves them money, improves their performance, and allows them to work more efficiently. Rather than pushing a one-size-fits-all solution for their clients, Segue customizes solutions based on the specific needs of each of their clients.

Ron Novak, Segue Technologies' executive vice president, discusses the changes Segue has made over the years to their marketing efforts and business model (going from just business-to-government [B2G] to business-to-business [B2B]) as they continue to stay at the forefront of the IT solutions industry.

> Initially, we started off doing Windows-based desktop development, mostly for procurement software and budgeting software for the Air Force. As technology changed rapidly, we moved to doing web application development and branched off into doing commercial as well, and then expanded from working with just the Air Force to working with the Marine Corps, Navy, and Army.

For a couple of years, Segue was comfortable growing their business strictly through the Armed Services sectors. However, during a time of government budget cuts, Segue realized (as many did in the B2G space) that in order to continue growing and evolving, they would have to branch out into the commercial space as well.

Says Novak:

> It was almost like an experiment just to see if we could even do commercial work. Fortunately, we ended up landing some pretty large clients. We started working with Sprint, Five Guys, and the United Negro College Fund. We had some good diversification at that point, which allowed us to kind of weather the storm during the government sequestration.

Novak quickly realized that doing business in the commercial space was quite different from doing business in the government space. Rather than through advertising, most of the business they had solicited from the federal government came via word of mouth and attending networking events.

> Before 2008, it was almost exclusively word-of-mouth, organic growth, and networking events. Doing business in the government space is a lot different than in the commercial world, so a lot of our marketing was just in-person networking and relationship building.

Like many companies, Segue Technologies had a business website, but they hadn't really been utilizing it. Novak realized the value a solid, evolving website and blog could add to the business if they were going to enter the commercial space with any success.

> We were slightly ahead of the curve of the defense contractors in that we actually saw the value in having a good website and having good content. But we really didn't know what good content meant for a long time. Even though we wrote some blogs back then, they were very inconsistent. We were lucky to do one or two a month, and we didn't really have a strategy behind the content we created, as it certainly wasn't close to aligning with They Ask, You Answer.

Although Segue had been taking a little time to try and bolster their website traffic through blogging, they weren't seeing the results they had hoped for.

> We were still growing—we were growing every year, but a lot of that was because of organic growth in our normal customer base. But very rarely did we get new customers coming to our website. We would get interest and maybe some decent leads every once in a while, but we didn't close many leads from the web. It was kind of one of those things that you really had to have a good website on the commercial side more than the government side.
>
> A lot of organizations in the [Department of Defense] space don't really think that your website is that important, and they still don't. It's still kind of an antiquated world in many ways, so I viewed it as a huge opportunity to differentiate ourselves from other competitors in our space and start to establish ourselves as thought leaders in our industry.

Novak was attending an event in the summer of 2012 when he heard me discuss the power of content, transparency, and They Ask, You Answer.

It was during Marcus's presentation that I had kind of a "light-bulb" moment. The first thing I thought was, "Man, I feel stupid. I should have been doing this years ago," as we'd had a website up for over ten years, and I couldn't believe we hadn't been doing this. It's crazy because it's so simple. The connection of answering people's questions is such a simple concept. But executing it was something that we had just never done before.

So, in January 2013, I met with much of Novak's company and introduced to the team the philosophy of They Ask, You Answer and the potential impact it could have on the company as a whole as well as the individuals, assuming everyone embraced this "teacher's mentality." Novak has since attributed that workshop as the pivotal moment when Segue Technologies' online efforts, and entire business model, began to shift.

After the workshop, Novak showed just how serious he was about this new philosophy by making it mandatory that every employee in the company contribute to the company's content strategy.

Each employee was tasked with writing at least one blog per quarter for a total of four blog posts per year.

We wanted to get everyone involved. Whether they were going to be great writers, or whether they were going to be people who were going to do it long term, I just wanted to at least try it.

Obviously, we had some people that took to it and enjoyed it. We had some people who didn't enjoy it as much, and others who may have not loved it, but saw the value of it, especially once their articles started ranking and we started getting leads from their articles.

The Snowball Begins

Within a short time, Segue's newly focused content marketing efforts began to pay off in ways they had always hoped they would. The early success they found inspired the team at Segue to continue to strengthen and develop their newfound obsession with educating their customers.

We had some pretty quick growth. Before we started this process we had [fewer] than 1,000 visitors a month to our website, and within three months of the workshop we had over 30,000.

We had several articles rank at number one on Google within a couple of months, so that really got people energized. For me it was just kind of a no-brainer from the beginning, but actually seeing it happen—watching the leads increase, and not just the number of leads, but the quality of leads as we improved our funnel and optimized our lead pages—was amazing.

It's been really fun to see it all evolve.

Segue Technologies' Astounding Growth

As Segue Technologies continued their content marketing efforts, they began to adjust their focus from simply getting articles out online to curating specific messages that they wanted to get across to their most ideal potential customers.

We got to the point where we had to tweak our contact pages, because we were getting so many leads, and not all of them were the right fit for us. Just the sheer quantity of traffic and leads was blown through the roof. All of that traffic allowed us to be a little more choosy, too.

For instance, one of the things we did was to change our contact form. Where it asks for them to give the size of their budget for their projects, we actually raised all of our values on them so that we could hone in a little closer to our ideal customers. We added additional questions as well. What it did was reduce the number of leads, but the quality of the leads kept getting better and better.

Improving the System to Produce Content

After they had amassed a large number of articles, Segue changed the method of how content was produced. They took things a step further and began to refine some of their older posts and ebooks with higher quality in mind.

When we first started producing content, we had an intern we had brought on specifically to help curate, organize, edit, and make sure the publishing schedule was staying on track. And she was amazing and has continued to do really great things for us, so we promoted her to content marketing manager. She's the one in charge for really keeping it going. It's important to have a person in that type of role.

We became a little bit looser on the number of articles everybody had to write, because we had developed quite a bit of content over the past few years, so we started focusing on refining the message.

We may not be producing as many blog articles per month as we used to, but we're much more thoughtful about what we're writing about, and we're doing a really good job of going back to older content and updating them, and updating the subsequent ebooks as we have a whole ebook strategy around our different service areas.

And because we started doing that, we've seen huge gains not only in traffic, but in the quality of leads, especially over the last six months.

Many businesses may think that targeting only specific types of leads could hurt their business by reducing traffic and overall lead generation, but Segue views their new efforts as exponentially valuable.

What's different about us is that we're not a business that brings in a ton of new clients each year, especially in the commercial space. If we bring on four or six new clients each year, that's actually a lot, because the size of our business deals are pretty large. *A typical deal for us is anywhere from a quarter million to a million dollars.*

When companies truly understand the power of great content and the philosophy of They Ask, You Answer, they don't just stop at using their content to attract visitors to their site, they continually repurpose their content at every step of the sales funnel.

Whether it's through emails, phone calls, webinars, or training, companies like Segue recognize the value their content has in guiding potential clients through the buyer's journey.

One surprising area [where] we've been able to utilize content is during "proposal season," which occurs every July and August. During this season, the government—and the DOD, in particular—have a lot of money they have to obligate and execute before the end of the government fiscal year, which is September 30.

It tends to be a very busy time, and when we're responding to requests for proposals, we'll use content created in our blogs to help us with proposals, because we've already thought about the questions and addressed the answers. Using content that we had already created previously as part of our proposals really helped us flesh them out and get them finished quicker.

Another factor that has helped Segue separate themselves from the rest of the pack in their industry is that they've never shied away from producing the types of articles that addressed questions their competitors weren't willing to answer, specifically, The Big 5 mentioned in Chapter 9.

It may not seem very bold now, but back in 2013, one of the first articles I wrote was, "How Much Does It Cost to Build a Mobile App?" Within two weeks that article ranked number 1 on Google.

Since then, others have written about it, but at the time, no one was willing to talk about it. We've also done a whole series of articles that sparked somewhat of a battle between our lead IOS developer for Apple and an Android developer for Google Apps with a number of articles that addressed the question, "Which is better?"

Other content has sparked quite a bit of back-and-forth debate in our comments sections. The article "Waterfall vs. Agile: Which Is the Right Development Methodology for Your Project?" got a lot of people from both sides sharing some very strong opinions.

With all of this, Segue continues to build its brand as one of the premier educators and thought leaders in their field. Today, they continue to set themselves apart from their respective peers by staying at the forefront of their industry, all thanks to their commitment to this business philosophy. And the numbers produced from their efforts prove that they're going to continue leading the pack for quite some time.

When we first started doing inbound marketing and They Ask, You Answer, we were getting around 1,000 visits to the website each month. Last month we had 85,000. And when we started tracking all of the revenue that could directly be attributed from inbound marketing, *it came out to $8,053,442.31.* And that's just since 2013. So I think that's a pretty cool inbound story.

Eight million in additional revenue?!
Yes, that is a cool story.

Well done, Ron Novak and Segue Technologies.

13

The Big 5, Topic 2

Problems: How to Turn Weaknesses into Strengths

Now that we've covered the first subject of The Big 5—or the five content subjects that move the needle in every industry, let's move to the second one: **problems**.

You may be thinking, *"What do you mean by 'problems,' Marcus?"*

Well, the simple answer is this: When people buy, they worry more about what might go wrong than about what will go right. It's true.

It is for this reason that, for example, when someone is buying a 2017 Ford Mustang, his or her main searches would be either "2017 Ford Mustang reviews" or "2017 Ford Mustang negative reviews."

But what they would *not* search is "***positive*** reviews 2017 Ford Mustang."

Make sense? In fact, I'd venture to say as a consumer you've searched by this point in your life hundreds of "negative"-based phrases, but no positives.

As buyers, although we want to know the good, bad, and ugly, we are mostly concerned with the ugly.

The same was true for me as a pool guy. Let's imagine for a minute that you had met with me back when I was a pool guy, and you had received a quote for a fiberglass swimming pool. Let's say you liked me as well as my pools, and you decided you might just want to buy one. But just to keep me honest, you elected to get a quote from a second swimming pool company—a concrete pool company. Let's call this company Concrete Joe's Pools.

Once you meet with Concrete Joe and tell him you met with Marcus, the fiberglass swimming pool guy, what do you think he's going to say about my fiberglass pools?

Of course, Concrete Joe is going to make such statements as:

- *"Fiberglass pools aren't wide enough or long enough or deep enough."*
- *"You can't customize them." Or "They crack." Or "They pop out of the ground."*
- *"You don't want a fiberglass pool! They are not even real pools. It's like having a bathtub in your yard!"*

And finally, he'll likely say something like: "If you buy a fiberglass pool, you're going to have nothing but problems, problems, problems. Don't get that pool if you don't want those problems!"

You might think I'm exaggerating with this scenario, but it's true. I saw it hundreds of times during my years selling swimming pools.

And when it does happen, as the buyer, you now have a moral dilemma. You liked me and you liked my pools, but after talking with Concrete Joe, you're a little freaked out worrying about all their potential problems.

What do you do next?

Sure, you may ask a friend, but what you're most likely going to do is go to Google and search something like, "fiberglass pool problems."

14

Addressing the Elephant in the Room

Since my first days as a fiberglass pool guy, one of the questions I heard for years was: *"Marcus, be honest with me. What are the problems with a fiberglass swimming pool?"*

And for years, just as I had done with the cost question, I danced around the answer. But once we embraced the philosophy of They Ask, You Answer, I said to myself, *"Enough is enough."* That led to my business partner, Jason, writing what turned out to be an epic article on the website titled: "Top 5 Fiberglass Pool Problems and Solutions."

Now you might think it would be insane for us to write an article with that title and, believe me, so did many people in our industry. But look at it this way: How many of our competitors were addressing that question on their websites? *Zero.*

Yet, how many consumers were wanting to know the answer to said question? *Pretty much all of them.*

The reason for these clear efforts to ignore such a question comes down to a psychological issue that almost all businesses struggle with, and that's the concept of addressing the elephant in the room.

Herein lies one of the great dilemmas of the digital age: ***Consumers are not dumb; nor are they ignorant.***

If the marketplace believes (rightfully or not) that a product, service, brand, or other factor has problems—they're very likely going to find out.

As a business, you have a choice:

- You can allow the consumer to discover your elephant(s) themselves and in turn lose trust in you.
- Or the minute they walk in the front door (or the virtual front door), you can say, *"Here's our elephant. Do you have a problem with it?"*

When we wrote this article, we said:

You know what? Buying a fiberglass swimming pool might not be for you. It might not be wide enough, or long enough, or deep enough. You might not be able to customize it to the extent that you want. But if you're looking for a low maintenance pool that is going to last you a lifetime and you like one of the shapes and sizes that we offer, well then a fiberglass pool might be the perfect choice for you.

15

How Talking About Our Problems Generated More Than $1 Million in Revenue

The reaction to the problems post on our website was very similar to the reaction we received from our cost piece. In both cases, consumers expressed their gratitude and ultimately gave us their trust. Just as before, if they could have responded with their voices, they might have said, *"Finally, **somebody** was willing to address this question!"*

What was the result of that post? Well, over the past ten years, more than 500,000 people have visited our website because their search criteria related to "problems" with fiberglass pools.

And thanks to the fact that we can track each visitor who eventually filled out a "Request a Quote" form, we also know this one article has generated well over $1 million in additional sales since the day it was published.

You may be wondering how talking about one's own problems (flaws, negative reviews, and such) could generate a million dollars, but the answer is simple really.

People trusted us because we were willing not only to address but to embrace the elephant in the room.

And that, in and of itself, is power.

In closing, I ask you this: *How many times over the years have prospective customers questioned you about any of the potential problems or issues they may experience with your products, services, or company?*

If they have asked you these types of questions, I guarantee you that thousands of others have searched those same issues online. I can also promise you that they are getting their answers from somewhere.

Wouldn't it be better if they were getting those answers from **you**?

Putting It into Action

Turn Your Problems into Strengths

This activity, like the others we've done up to this point, will not work unless you're truly in tune with the way your prospects and customers think. Nor will it work if you're not completely honest with your answers.

To start, answer the following two (very related) questions:

- What does the competition say is a negative about the thing we sell?
- What do consumers and buyers see as the negatives of our products and services? (Is it that you're the most expensive? Is your product only a good fit for certain applications?)

Once you've completed this, ask yourself:

- "How can we address each of these honestly and transparently on our website and within our sales process to turn it into an advantage?"

Assuming you approach this the right way, the answer to this question (and the actions you take) could lead to some pretty incredible results for your brand and business.

16 | Case Study 2

An Equipment Financing Company Becomes a Digital David and Conquers the Industry Goliaths

Another tremendous success story of They Ask, You Answer—especially when addressing the "problems" of an industry—comes from Rob Misheloff of Smarter Finance USA.

In a couple of years, Misheloff has worked wonders to transform his one-man financial loan information company into an inbound lead and sales-generating powerhouse, all the while becoming a digital David in a land of financial Goliaths and proving himself more nimble, fast, and creative than his behemoth counterparts.

Approaching his website content with a unique blend of helpful information, bold transparency, and more than a dash of his own brand of humor, Misheloff has been successful not only in educating his clients and growing his business, but he's been having a good time doing it, too.

And like many who share similar success stories in the world of great content, Misheloff just kind of stumbled into it.

About Smarter Finance USA

Misheloff got his start back in 2003 when he formed a small reverse-mortgage direct mail company that sent out mailers to elderly people who were "house rich, but cash poor."

He loved his job because he felt that he was making a difference in peoples' lives by offering them a chance to access their home equity while deferring mortgage payments until after their death. With reverse mortgages, elderly clients "no longer had to make the tough decisions of choosing between food and medicine, even though they owned their house," says Misheloff. However, in 2013, changes to the product Misheloff was selling made it less viable, and Misheloff was left scrambling to find a new business.

Because direct mail had worked so well for him in the past, he believed that he just needed to find a new market in which he could easily create a niche for himself.

Through a former employee, he heard about the equipment financing industry. But when Misheloff started digging into the financing trade to learn more about competitors already in the field, he found something quite disturbing.

> One of the things I loved about my direct mailing business was that it was in an industry where most of our customers were really good people and they wanted the best for their clients. There were very few charlatans. We found that in the equipment financing industry from listening to our customers that *they were just being lied to by brokers and lenders*. These other companies knew that guys driving trucks didn't really know finance, so they could just tell them anything.

Misheloff wanted to be in a business that truly helped people solve their problems, and he "wasn't going to be in a business to help others steal from small business owners."

With this desire at heart, Misheloff made the decision to start Smarter Finance USA in January 2014. This new company would help people who wanted to finance equipment for small businesses by giving them as much information as they needed to make informed financial decisions.

However, Misheloff quickly realized that his old tactics of using direct mail to solicit new leads just wasn't as effective as it had been in the reverse-mortgage world he had previously occupied. And so, like many startup companies looking to stake their claims in a new trade, Misheloff took to the web.

> I got started at the end of January 2014 and realized I needed to get some leads. I first tried some spam e-mails—they didn't work so well. Then I turned to PPC [pay per click/Google Ads], which were a little successful in generating leads, but not really worth the price I was paying per click. With this method, I was able to get people to a one-page landing page and try to work the leads from there, but it's really hard to quickly earn the trust of someone trying to get a loan, especially because these people know absolutely nothing about you or your business.

Smarter Finance USA Embraces They Ask, You Answer

The philosophies of They Ask, You Answer came to Misheloff completely by chance as he was up late one night and saw a link someone had posted of Marcus Sheridan's ebook, *Inbound and Content Marketing Made Easy*. With his wife and daughter asleep, Misheloff figured a quick look at the book couldn't hurt anything.

> I actually ended up reading the entire book that night. It was the first time in my life I had ever read a book and said "This is literally going to change my life." And I didn't even know why I had so much faith, but I did. I just knew this was for me.

Within days, Misheloff and I were on the phone discussing his goals and planning out a strategy that would, in many ways, make him the kingpin of his space.

The principles of content marketing and They Ask, You Answer really spoke to Misheloff because they epitomized what he had felt all along, and what he found to be missing among his peers in his industry: *He wanted to bring truth and honesty back into online financing information.*

And he planned to do it better than anybody had before.

Misheloff didn't want to simply find financial success. He is one of those rare types who genuinely wants to help people in difficult situations get the best care they can, so that they have a shot at building a successful small business of their own.

Smarter Finance USA Focuses on Educating Small Business Owners Searching for Equipment Loans Online

Among the first pieces of content that Misheloff wrote were those aimed at dispelling the dishonesty found in so many of his competitors' rate quotes and to carefully explain to readers how they could avoid being scammed while searching for equipment loans.

He focused on articles that explained the pros and cons of leasing equipment and how people can easily spot a loan scam, and he wrote other articles that detailed the problems with the leasing industry in general.

Here are a few examples:

- "A Review of Go Capital: Are They Legit?"
- "5 Ways to Get Out of a Merchant Cash Advance (and Other Toxic Business Loans)"
- "5 Lies Heavy Equipment Financing Companies Tell You"
- "5 Restaurant Equipment Leasing Swindles to Avoid"
- "Gym Equipment Leasing: True Costs of Fitness Equipment Financing"
- "An Honest Review of One of the Best Truck Factoring Companies"
- "Private Business Loans: 5 Secrets the Big Boys Hope You Never Learn"
- "Contractor Loans: 7 Ways to Finance Your Construction Business"
- "Small Business Term Loan vs. Merchant Cash Advance: Which Is Best?"
- "Daily Payment Loans for Your Business: Do They Ever Make Sense?"

It's such a dirty industry. It's unregulated, and so people will outright lie to customers. You can even find it on the front page of Google. Some of the biggest companies in the industry always start by saying, "Our rates are 5 percent." But almost none of the people shopping online for equipment financing are ever going to qualify for a 5 percent rate. For a small business owner shopping online for financing, those rates almost never exist.

With such focus on exposing truth versus scams, Misheloff gained more and more respect from consumers for his willingness to address the industry's elephants, and in that process, he gained a phenomenal amount of trust. In fact, it became quite common that people would reach out to Misheloff after reading his articles on scams and then send him the contracts they'd received from leasing companies to ask if the contract looked fair.

"I see some of these contracts and they're total garbage designed to steal from people," says Misheloff. "It's really disgusting that this happens in my industry."

Misheloff has made it his mission to set the record straight about equipment leasing online, and in just a little more than two years has produced hundreds of articles and videos detailing how people can find financing for a wide variety of equipment.

Whether he's writing about how to found financing for dump trucks, limousines, food trucks, welding equipment, arcade games, forklifts, chiropractic equipment, or any other equipment for which a small business may need to find financing, Misheloff works hard to make sure that his content is thorough, informative, transparent, and even humorous at times.

He also prides himself on the fact that, while some content marketers claim to knock out entire articles every day, he can spend up to three days working on a single piece of content. But he does it with the assurance that it's going to "be the best stuff that's out there."

> I take subjects that have very low keyword value (aren't necessarily searched by many people), and make these huge articles out of them. I have multiple infographics that I make myself, and I add videos, and all kinds of other crazy stuff, because I figure that each article I write is going to produce leads for years. I'm not writing the articles for just right now, because right now it's actually kind of easy to rank for a lot of these things in Google because my competitors are still doing it the way they've always done it.
>
> But I know in a few years these same competitors will start to figure out that they really need to be producing content and answering consumer questions themselves, but by the time they get with the times, it's going to be tough to knock me off the hill, regardless of how large they are as an organization.

Smarter Finance USA's Educational Content Pays Off in a Big Way

The proof of Misheloff's efforts lies in the growth that he has experienced in both traffic and in leads. In his first two years, Misheloff's site has doubled nearly every two to three months in traffic, starting with just a few hundred visits at the beginning to more than 25,000 visits in late 2015. During this time, he amassed more than 2,600 new contacts who have taken the time to fill out a form on his website.

Misheloff himself was even stunned by the number of leads he was getting every month and shortly realized that he wouldn't be able to work every deal himself.

> For the most part, I don't even work the leads anymore. I get over 500 leads a month just from the website and another hundred or two in phone calls. I don't have my own team, so what I do is farm the leads out to a few different companies that I think are the best fit for the types of leads I'm getting.

When asked about specific return on investment (ROI) Misheloff stated:

> January 2015 (about six months in) was when I saw my first dollar of revenue from all the work I was doing.
>
> First quarter of 2015, I ended up closing six transactions totaling $220,000 in funding, resulting in $11,846 revenue. Not a lot, but this was enough to validate that money *could* be made.
>
> First quarter of 2016, 30 transactions, $2,045,000 in funding, resulting in $144,112 in revenue. A good chunk of that revenue is shared with affiliates, but what I am taking home for the first quarter of 2016 is about $55,000 in profit.

Misheloff knows that if he hired more staff and rented out a legitimate workspace he could broker most the deals in-house and keep the lion's share of the profit. But Misheloff is more concerned about maintaining the lifestyle that he has come to know and love.

> When you're not paying for the leads, you have to ask yourself: "Am I more interested in maximizing my profits, or my happiness?" And for me, the answer is, "I just want to do it the inbound way."
>
> I don't want to open an office, or have a large staff, or spend my day talking into a phone, or have to drive into work every day. I get to work from home in shorts and a T-shirt. I don't have any stress; I don't have anything to worry about.

And not only that, but Misheloff, unlike many businesses, has always seen his size (or lack thereof) as a major advantage when embracing the digital consumer. Instead of all the red tape that typically comes with working for larger organizations, if he wants to talk about something, he talks about it. If he wants to get something done, he does it.

Up to the present day, Misheloff continues to dominate his space as a one-man army, and his joy is palpable.

> You hear people saying how tough it is to make it on the internet, and that you have to be some mega corporation to be successful—it's all crap! Just obsess over your customer. Figure out what they're thinking, asking, and going through. Then have the guts to address it. This philosophy has made me who I am and offered me an extraordinary lifestyle in the process.

An extraordinary lifestyle and an even more extraordinary example of what one person can do despite an incredibly competitive niche. All in a day's work for Rob Misheloff.

17

The Big 5, Topic 3

Versus and Comparisons

The third major content subject of The Big 5 is that of "versus" and/or "comparisons." As consumers, we're *fascinated* with comparisons. We love knowing the best, the worst, and everything in between. And having all the information in the world at our fingertips has made this thirst even more prominent.

Think about the last major purchase you made—were you looking only at one option or multiple? If you're like most buyers, before you made the purchasing decision you researched multiple options, ultimately making your decision after stacking them up against each other and then choosing the one that you felt was best for your needs.

But you're not alone. Hundreds of thousands of comparisons are searched online every single day.

When I was a pool guy, the story was no different. In fact, our biggest competition wasn't other fiberglass pool builders, but rather concrete or vinyl-liner, in-ground swimming pool companies. Because fiberglass was "the new kid on the block," other pool companies would continually criticize it, claiming it was flawed, inferior, cheap, "not a real pool," and so on.

Over the years, one of the top questions I received from potential customers was, *"OK, Marcus, why would I get a fiberglass pool over concrete?"*

73

For a long time, like most pool builders, I didn't address this question on our company website. We simply talked about fiberglass, and that was it. In hindsight, this was really, *really* dumb.

I can't even imagine how many potential customers dismissed us because they had received wrong or inaccurate information from another source. Furthermore, I don't know how many hours I had wasted on the phone and in person with shoppers who clearly were not a good fit for fiberglass. But because they didn't know any better, their time—and my time—were wasted.

Once we embraced They Ask, You Answer as a company, it became obvious we needed to address this major question. But what really pushed us over the edge was the following email we received from a reader of the website:

> As you're no doubt well aware, it's a desert wasteland when trying to find information on pools ... sorting through the internet for usable information is difficult in the extreme. Of the few forums I've found, most devolve into trolls arguing gunite (concrete) vs. fiberglass vs. vinyl liner— over and over and over and over.
>
> What would help a great deal is to find some kind of unbiased information that explains each pool in detail and then backs off—letting me (or the customer) make the final decision.

Finally, after receiving this email and hearing the same question hundreds of times over the years, we produced an article on our website entitled, "Fiberglass Pools vs. Vinyl Liner Pools vs. Concrete Pools: An Honest Comparison."

Once again, we were the first in our space to address the question.

And why were we first?

Again, companies were focused more on their own fears and inadequacies rather than on what buyers really wanted to know.

To justify their actions, fiberglass pool builders were literally using the following logic:

"Our biggest competition is concrete swimming pools. So, to deal with this problem, we're not even going to discuss concrete pools on our website. And if we don't discuss them on our website, no one will know they exist."

Yes, you did just read that correctly. And yes, that was the logic of fiberglass pool builders for years—and still, for many, to this day.

But as you can surely imagine, this example in the swimming pool space is replicated and followed in just about every other industry in the world. It's what we all do—a classic case of ostrich marketing.

We think if we ignore the problem (or question) that it will go away, but it doesn't. And ignoring it only destroys trust.

Remember: *Consumer ignorance is no longer a viable sales and marketing strategy.*

If we're counting on the idea that a prospect or customer isn't going to find out about another option, sale, discount, brand, technology, methodology, or other factor, then we're sorely mistaken.

Just because consumers might start out as ignorant (not informed), eventually they will become informed buyers. In fact, many will get to a place where they're even more informed than the vendor or salesperson they're dealing with.

It's a reality of the digital age.

And because of this reality, we have to live and do business by a different standard.

We must say to ourselves: *"Let's assume our prospects and customers know every single other possible solution, possible vendor, and possible competitor out there."*

If we conduct our business that way, and design all of our sales and marketing messaging to be aligned with this philosophy, the possibilities are literally endless.

The Results

So what was the result of honestly comparing all types of swimming pools?

Well, as you likely already guessed, searchers (consumers) and search engines alike absolutely loved the content. As a company, we have received hundreds of compliments from swimming pool shoppers over the years, expressing just how thrilled they were to finally read an "unbiased" review of the different types of pools. And with more informed shoppers who were able to truly understand the differences between the types of pools, we have received dramatically fewer phone calls and gone on way fewer appointments of "bad-fit" prospects—those for whom a fiberglass pool was clearly not the best option.

Along with this success, the search engines once again rewarded our willingness to address supposedly "difficult" questions. To this day, our website is the first to show up in a Google search engine results page when you type in:

- Fiberglass vs. concrete pools
- Fiberglass vs. vinyl pools
- Vinyl vs. concrete pools
- Concrete compared to fiberglass pools
- Concrete compared to vinyl liner pools
- Etc.

That one article has generated hundreds of thousands of dollars in revenue since the day it was written. But it is just one of many comparison-based pieces of content we've produced over the years, all because we've been asked so many times, *"So tell me the difference between ..."*

Putting It into Action

Write down every question you've ever received from a prospect or customer who was asking you to compare two or more things. This could include products, brands, methods, companies, and other subjects. It could also include your products and services or ones you don't even sell.

The key, though, is that you consider the many comparison-based questions that potential buyers and customers are asking (and searching) in your industry right now.

Once you've made this list, address these questions honestly and transparently throughout your digital marketing efforts—be it with blog posts, videos, buying guides, webinars, and so on.

18 | The Critical Need for Unbiased Content

Whenever I've taught audiences about the need to address the comparison-based questions we continually hear from customers, someone will inevitably say something like "It's impossible for businesses to address that type of question well. They're biased, and consumers know it."

Let me simply say this statement is fundamentally false.

Consumers *do* want to know what your business believes about these types of questions; otherwise, they wouldn't ask you the question in the first place.

But the response you give them... now that's where you have to overcome this incessant need to brag, exaggerate, and only focus on why your company (or product, service, and so on) is the greatest thing since sliced bread.

How do you do it? How do you immediately gain the reader's (or viewer's) trust while overcoming this hurdle of sounding biased? Well, let's go back to the example of writing an article (or producing a video—the process doesn't change) that compares fiberglass, concrete, and vinyl-liner pools. If you're going to write an article like this, the proper way to do it might sound something like this:

Each year customers come to us at River Pools and ask us, "What is the difference between a concrete and a fiberglass pool?"

This is a very good question. We can certainly understand the need to know the difference, as it is a choice pool buyers are going to have to live with as long as they're in their home.

At River Pools, we only sell fiberglass pools, but the truth of the matter is, a fiberglass pool might not be the best fit for you. In fact, a concrete or vinyl-liner pool might be the better option.

This article is going to explain the pros and cons of each type of swimming pool in an honest and transparent manner. This way, by the end, you'll be able to identify which is the best fit for *you*.

Disarmament: The Quickest Way to Build Trust

The principle at work in the opening you just read is a principle we've used many times with our clients all over the world, the principle of *disarmament,* which is arguably the least understood element of great communication and copy—online and offline.

To understand the principle of disarmament, imagine you are negotiating in a hostage situation. As a trained negotiator, the first thing you ask the gunman to do (in most cases) is to put his weapon down.

We've all heard this phrase in movies, but believe it or not, it has serious significance in the world of sales and marketing, too.

In a hostage situation, unless someone puts his weapons down, it's almost impossible to communicate with him, much less earn his trust. But once he does put the weapon down, the process of negotiation (trust-building) can begin.

It's much the same with sales and marketing communication—in order to make progress and earn trust, especially when the buyer senses the business is biased, disarmament is a must.

For example, if I were going to write an article comparing fiberglass and concrete swimming pools (as shown previously), I must first eliminate the elephant(s) in the room, and I would do this by:

- First stating that our company sells *only* fiberglass pools.
- Immediately admitting that fiberglass isn't necessarily the best choice for everyone.
- Stating that concrete pools might, at times, be the better option.

■ Explaining how the article (or video) takes an honest look at the pros and cons of each, allowing readers to decide the best choice for themselves.

When you come out of the gate and mention these things, the reader will immediately sense the honesty (and sheer uniqueness) within the company or brand, and therefore place more trust in what is being said.

You should always look for examples of what is good about the *other* choice or option when explaining things to your prospects and customers. If you're willing to give them both sides of the coin, they will see you as the trustworthy voice. And they are going to think: *"This person truly does have my best interests at heart."*

That is the essence of disarmament.

Let me again stress, though, that disarmament goes well beyond the things you say on your company website. Essentially, it's the way we approach customer questions with our business, be it face-to-face, online, or in other situations.

For example, let's examine an offline scenario.

Imagine you're in a sales situation and you've just made your pitch to the prospect. You've spent a good bit of time explaining all your company's features, benefits, deliverables, results, and so on. She's seen your proposal and is at the point of making a decision. But before she gives you the *"Yes!"* you seek, she leans back in her chair, folds her arms (the classic defensive position), and asks one more question:

"OK, you've explained all this to me very well, but I have one last question. Why should I choose your company?"

Ninety-nine percent of the time, sales professionals who hear such a question would immediately go into why they (company, product, solution, and so on) are the best. But the truly elite communicators understand the defensive nature of this question and know that this is exactly what the person who asked the question expects to hear.

The best response to disarm such a question is quite the opposite:

Well, to be completely frank with you, we may not be the best choice for you. We have been talking about your needs and your situation and describing what we can bring to the table to address those needs. You have also done this with other companies. You've seen their prices and you've seen ours. That means that, by now, you probably have a pretty good feel for things. So the question is, Do you, based on what you've now heard, feel we are the best option for you?

The answer that comes next will be dramatically more telling than any further pitch would ever be for the prospect. As buyers and consumers, we don't want to be told what to do or what to buy. Rather, we want to think we've educated ourselves enough to arrive at an informed conclusion.

The best sales teams and companies in the digital age understand and embrace this reality.

19

The Big 5, Topics 4 and 5

Reviews and Best in Class

Before we dive into the powerful elements of this chapter, let me just mention that what you're about to read is a very, very different way of approaching business and consumer education than what most people are used to. It's not taught in MBA programs, and it's certainly not the norm.

But that, in and of itself, should make it a good thing. After all, the most successful business innovations of the digital age happen time and time again when an organization elects to take the road less traveled, ultimately clearing a new path and a new way of seeing "the way it should be done."

And with that, we'll now discuss the final two elements of The Big 5: *reviews* and *best in class*.

As stated in the previous chapter, as consumers and buyers we love to compare. We love knowing whom everyone else loves, hates, and how they all stack up against each other. We're also obsessed with reviews.

Whether it's a website like Yelp, Angie's List, or even a print publication like *Motor Trend*'s Car of the Year, we are a society that cares about pecking order.

After embracing They Ask, You Answer in 2009, as a business owner I started to look at the types of content that were experiencing success in multiple industries and I came to an interesting conclusion: *There was no Yelp or* Motor Trend *Car of the Year award for the fiberglass swimming pool industry.*

Notwithstanding, ours was very similar to the car industry. A handful of manufacturers make shells of pools. They're like the Toyota, Ford, or Chevy of the fiberglass pool sector. They manufacture and distribute their shells to the hundreds and hundreds of pool installers all over the world. And most installers, like us at River Pools and Spas, carry one or two of these brands at a time—competing with the rest in the space, just as in the auto industry.

But I noticed that if a consumer wanted to know who the best manufacturers were, there was no authority there to tell him. Also, if a consumer wanted to know the best models and shapes these manufacturers were building, again, there was nothing in the market that was designed to help.

It was during this time that my mind shifted back to the core principles of They Ask, You Answer and I thought:

"Consumers want to see these types of ranking systems. And they certainly want to know the best swimming pool shapes and sizes for their needs. Therefore, if they want them, it's my job to give it to them."

And that's exactly what we did. In early 2011, I experimented with this type of content when I published an article entitled "The Best Fiberglass Pool Design Awards for 2011."

To come up with this piece, I spent hours getting to know the different manufacturers in our space. I looked at all their pool designs, focusing my attention on the various shapes, sizes, and unique features. Next, I divided all of these designs into different classes, such as "Best Kidney Pool," "Best Free-Form Pool," "Best Diving Pool," and so on.

Once this was done, I formulated the article, naming the various manufacturers I truly felt were "best in class" of that particular shape.

Although this may not sound that innovative, keep in mind that the very manufacturers I was giving out "best in class" awards to were the same ones I was selling against every day as an installer.

Without reading any further, can you guess how these manufacturers reacted when this article was posted online? Needless to say, they were very surprised, and reactions were mixed. Many of those who were included on the list contacted me, thanking me for the inclusion.

Others who were not included on the list called me and said things like: *"Marcus, I see we are not on your list of the best pool shapes in class. Why don't you come out to our facility and see our fiberglass pools?"*

I'm sure there were others who did not contact me at all, but the end result was the same for each. Before the day this article was published, I wasn't anywhere on their radar. Frankly, they didn't know me from Adam—I was just some 31-year-old kid who was part-owner of a little swimming pool company in Virginia.

But once I published my reviews in an open forum, and they saw people were paying attention, they couldn't help but take notice.

Even funnier, some of these manufacturers, upon receiving their awards, were announcing on the home pages of their websites that they had won a design award for best pool in class.

At the same time, my article was a hit with consumers. Finally, they were given something that would allow them to choose the right pool based on their individual wants and needs. The article was so successful that we've produced more like it every year, all with resounding success. All have continued to build the River Pools and Spas brand, authority, and trust with consumers.

Today, if you go online and search anything related to fiberglass pool designs, one of these articles will likely be the first thing you see in search engine results.

Even better, these articles have built hundreds of inbound links coming from other websites over the years, many of which are coming from the manufacturers we compete against on a daily basis.

Putting It into Action

Highlight Others and Build Your Referral Network

Contemplate ways to make reviews work for your company. Are there any "best of class" types of content you could produce in your industry? Remember, if you've ever been asked to compare two things, then the answer is very likely "Yes."

Also, consider all of the companies within your industry or a similar industry that could possibly be referral sources for your business.

Find ways, assuming they're respectable organizations with good track records, to highlight who they are, what they sell, and why they're respected in the marketplace.

The key here is that you see yourself as more than a subject matter expert within your industry, but as someone who sees outside of your small circle and therefore has an opinion, expertise, and knowledge of those subjects that matter most to the consumer.

20

Using Reviews to Establish Yourself as an Expert

Now that we've discussed how to build your referral network and industry authority by writing review-based content, let's look at an even more unorthodox (and shocking to some) approach to building your brand and business—one that demonstrates the essence of They Ask, You Answer.

Have you ever had a prospect say: *"We like you, and we expect we may do business with you, but in case we don't, is there anyone else you might be willing to recommend?"*

If you've been in business long enough, you've likely heard this question before. You also most likely know that when most companies receive such a question, the natural response is, "There is no one quite like us!"

When someone responds with a statement like that, you and I both know that the person asking the question is going to think, *"Oh, come on. Seriously?"*

Once, during my final year of selling swimming pools, I spent about two hours in a sales appointment with a couple. When I had finished giving them my proposal they said: *"Marcus, we really like you a lot. We do. And we think we're going to use you. But hypothetically speaking, if we don't use you, who would you recommend that we use?"*

Alas, the last thing you want to hear as a salesperson.

That night, I did not earn their business. But I did have a long drive home. And on that drive, I thought a lot about that question, as well as our rule of They Ask, You Answer. Upon reflection, I said to myself, *"Well, if they asked the question, I guess I need to answer it."*

When I arrived home at midnight, I immediately sat down at my kitchen table and wrote the article, "Who Are the Best Pool Builders in Richmond, Virginia (Reviews/Ratings)" and posted it to our site. I listed the five companies I believed were truly the best builders in Richmond.

Before I go any further, let me ask you: *Do you think I included myself (River Pools and Spas) in that list?*

If you answered "No," you are correct. Now, before you go on thinking I'm crazy, let's analyze why I wasn't on the list.

The first and obvious reason is that the moment I put myself on a "best of" list of any kind, I lose all credibility. Any trust I might have built with the prospective customer is now gone. And as we've established many times in this book, everything comes down to trust. So, no, I did not put myself on that list.

Furthermore, if someone starts reading that article, where is he or she? That's right—he or she is already on my site.

In other words, I don't need to prove that I'm awesome. Viewers can see it for themselves. They can figure it out very quickly whether they like me or not. And in this case, let's assume that you went online right now and typed into Google "Best Pool Builders Richmond, Virginia"—which is a very common search phrase for pool shoppers in that area.

Upon doing this, you'd immediately see this article (which is ranked first for the phrase in Google search engine results) and click to read more.

You would then commence reading the following:

Each year at River Pools and Spas, we meet with well over a hundred households in the Richmond area with respect to their in-ground swimming pool installation.

And because so many folks know our thoughts and feelings on all things related to pool construction from this website, they often ask us, "Who are some of the other builders and competitors in the area?"

Never one to shy away from being blatantly honest about the competition, here is a list of some of the companies that have a solid in-ground swimming pool building history in the Richmond area.

Many companies use every page of their website to try to convince viewers how superior and awesome they are. In reality, no one wants to hear (from you) that you're awesome. Rather, what buyers want is to look at your works, judge them, and then make their own decisions on just how great your company really is.

Now, you tell me—if you were a swimming pool shopper and read those first two paragraphs, what would your impression of the company be? Do they sound believable? Honest? In fact, could you go so far as to assume they might just be experts?

If you're like most people, you answered affirmatively to all three questions. Without the company needing to state it, you now feel like that they are experts and thought leaders—all because they've shown you they're willing to answer a question honestly and transparently, when no one else in their space is.

This goes back to what we talked about with disarmament, and this is the essence of great content and They Ask, You Answer:

Honesty and transparency are self-evident and, when done with the right intentions, have a profound influence on the business, brand, and bottom line.

21

The Impact
of Discussing
Competition

You may be wondering what the final results of "Who Are the Best Pool Builders in Richmond, Virginia (Reviews/Ratings)" are.

To put it lightly, the results have been profound.

First, as mentioned before, if you search anything to do with "Best Pool Builders Richmond, Virginia," this is generally the first result you see in Google.

But the second result is where things get really interesting.

Let's assume you went online today and searched for "Reviews Pla-Mor Pools Richmond, Virginia"—Pla-Mor is our biggest competitor in the Richmond area. Once you enter such a search query, one of the first results you're going see is that article.

In fact, today, whenever anyone is researching reviews of our competitors, they often land on one of these articles (as we've now produced many) on our website. All this has happened while outranking such websites as the Better Business Bureau, Angie's List, and others that often own the conversation about reviews in multiple industries, especially in-home improvement.

To put it all in perspective, allow me to share the following story of a lady who bought a swimming pool from us a few years ago.

Upon discussing her decision to go with our company, she said:

Marcus, the most interesting thing happened. I was so close to signing a contract with Pla-Mor Pools for my swimming pool. But before I signed the contract, I decided to go online and research their company. While I was researching their company, I immediately stumbled across this article you guys had written and thought to myself, *"My goodness, these guys are so honest, I should probably call them too!"*

Of course, you can probably guess what happened. That lady bought a $50,000 swimming pool from us. And she bought it all because she had a common question and we were the ones that had been willing to answer it—honestly and transparently.

The year it was published, that one little article resulted in $150,000 in sales. Still today, if you go online and research the best swimming pool builders in Richmond, Virginia, we will probably be one of the first companies you come across.

"Yeah, but Marcus, aren't you afraid you've now introduced them to the competition?"

If you're thinking this, let's be clear about something: If someone wants to know who your competitors are, roughly, how long will it take them to figure it out? Seconds, if they're slow!

The reality is this: *Consumer ignorance is no longer a viable sales and marketing strategy.*

It just isn't.

I knew at some point the buyer would learn about my competitors, just as I knew at some point they'd realize there are three types of in-ground pools (concrete, fiberglass, and vinyl). Plus, I could see how addressing these types of questions would give us a chance at doing business with folks who never would have found us otherwise—just as the lady who almost bought a Pla-Mor Pool had done. But because we had addressed the question, we were now able to enter the conversation with her and many, many others.

To this day, we are still being rewarded for taking this bold approach to They Ask, You Answer, with new business every single month.

And finally, if you're wondering how our competitors reacted to these articles, I can tell you that over the years, I've heard from many of them, and the response is almost always the same: *"Marcus, I don't know why you wrote that article, but thank you."*

As for me, all I can do is chuckle, knowing the simplistic power and impact of They Ask, You Answer.

Putting It into Action

Embrace Review-Based and "Best of" Content

Brainstorm the top competitors and companies in your space, and then take the time to write an article about the best companies in your field. Remember to stick to facts and stay away from opinions when discussing the competition on your own website. But the key here is your willingness to have the conversation and become the trusted source for your industry in the process.

22 | Case Study 3

Small Retail Appliance Store Dominates Online and Makes Millions

If you were asked which company you thought was the biggest online thought leader in the kitchen appliance space, you'd probably assume that it was one of the major manufacturers you've been seeing in kitchens for years. Names like General Electric, Whirlpool, Kenmore, and Frigidaire might come to mind. Worth hundreds of millions of dollars each, these companies, at least in theory, should "own" the digital space.

However, you might be surprised to learn that not only is the go-to consumer information source in the appliance space not one of the leading manufacturers, but it's not a manufacturer at all.

Rather, the company that is making a killing by providing educational articles, videos, buyer's guides, and ebooks that are answering people's questions about appliances is a regional retail store located in Boston.

About Yale Appliance

Yale Appliance has been selling and servicing the people of Boston with all of their home appliance and lighting purchases since 1923. From the Great Depression of the late 1920s and early 1930s, to the dotcom explosion of

the mid-90s and the Great Recession of 2008, Yale Appliance has perse-
vered through it all.

How does a local appliance store maintain such longevity while many
other businesses in their field have been forced to shutter their doors during periods of economic decline? *They turned to their customers and started
paying close attention to their habits, problems, and needs.*

Steve Sheinkopf, CEO of Yale Appliance, is a perfect example of a
business owner who caught on to content marketing at an early stage,
when he went to a conference called In Planet back in 2004.

> In Planet was the single greatest conference I've ever been to. HubSpot's
> conferences are amazing, but this one was really foretelling of the future.
> They were saying things like, "While social media isn't quite there yet for
> businesses, it soon will be."
>
> I also learned that the first thing a company needs to do is manage
> their reputation online, and the second thing is to find a way to control
> the conversation somehow.

In 2007, Sheinkopf decided it was time to take control of online
conversations about home appliances by starting a business blog for Yale
Appliance. He had always distrusted the measurability of traditional advertising, and he saw an opportunity with content marketing for a greater
return on his investment and the possibility to measure that return with
concrete numbers.

For four years, Sheinkopf was pleased with the online results he was
seeing—a growing social media presence as well as a steady (albeit slight)
uptick in monthly traffic.

As much as he personally despised traditional outbound advertising,
there were times when he believed that he had no choice but to turn to it.

> I've never been sold on advertising, even though we were doing some
> radio and television ads, and buying space in the *Boston Globe*. We
> were spending a lot of money. When the recession hit, I had read
> somewhere that refrigerators actually sold better during recessions
> like the Great Depression. So we advertised even more, but we didn't
> really get anything out of it.

The recession forced Sheinkopf to reevaluate his business goals
and plans.

When I was struggling during the recession, we had to ask ourselves the same two questions every other business has to: "How do I reduce expenses?" and "How do I add revenue?" And it usually boils down to the same answers: "I need to sell more, and I need to cut more." And that's really hard to do. Anybody with compassion hates to cut people.

It was during these tough economic times that Sheinkopf decided to explore further why his inbound marketing strategy wasn't producing the results he was after, so he turned to the web for answers.

A CEO Becomes Head of Business Development

Sheinkopf was reading articles about HubSpot when he stumbled across the River Pools story and decided to reach out to me to see whether my having a workshop with his employees could help turn around his company's inbound marketing efforts. But as he jokingly recalls, our first conversation didn't quite go as he had anticipated.

> My first talk with Marcus was brutal. I thought I was pretty good at business blogging, and I was just thinking that maybe I could improve a little bit. So I sent him a few articles for review and he kind of just beat me down.
>
> Marcus said to me, "I can see that you do the work, and that you take this seriously, but the truth of the matter is you're not doing it right. And we're not going to talk about what you're doing right, we're going to talk about what you're doing wrong, and how you can fix it. Can you handle that?" I almost hung up on him right then.

On a personal level, as the author of this book—and now someone who considers Sheinkopf a close friend—this statement gave me quite a laugh.

But the truth is, his content strategy was way off. It was almost the antithesis of They Ask, You Answer. Instead of focusing on what consumers were asking, thinking, and searching for about kitchen appliances, he was writing about everything from the business's point of view (and not the consumer's) and was therefore experiencing almost no momentum from his efforts.

(This, by the way, is extremely common for businesses all over the world when they embrace an inbound culture with content marketing. Although they are producing content, they are still doing it in a biased, sales-based manner versus one that is solely focused on teaching, helping, and solving another's problems.)

Fortunately, Steve ended up embracing my earnest criticism of Yale's content marketing efforts, and after a few further correspondences, he decided to have me come out to his company and teach content marketing in the style that had worked so well with our clients and River Pools: They Ask, You Answer.

After Yale Appliance's workshop in early 2011, Sheinkopf and his employees began tackling their content marketing strategy with a rejuvenated passion and a new purpose that consisted of a clear direction and attainable goals.

Part of Sheinkopf's new plan was to reevaluate his company's overall goals. He realized that in order to achieve those goals he would have to put the customers first, produce content that was helpful, and better aid clients in their purchasing decisions. Specifically, he focused on the Big 5 content topics and knew that if he was going to become something like a "Yelp for kitchen appliances," he was going to have to address the same types of subjects they did.

In fact, here is a list of just some of the extremely popular articles that Yale published since embracing this strategy, all of which have been viewed over 100,000 times each:

- "The 5 Best Counter Depth Refrigerators"
- "The Least Serviced/Most Reliable Appliance Brands 2015 (Reviews/ Ratings)"
- "The Best Compact Laundry for 2015 (Reviews/Ratings/Prices)"
- "Quietest Dishwasher by Decibel Rating (Reviews/Prices)"
- "The 5 Best Affordable Luxury Appliance Brands (Reviews/Ratings)"
- "KitchenAid vs. Bosch Dishwashers (Reviews/Ratings/Prices)"
- "Best Front-Load Washers for 2016 (Ratings/Reviews/Prices)"
- "The 5 Best Bosch Dishwashers (Ratings/Reviews/Prices)"
- "The Best Induction Cooktops for 2015 (Ratings/Reviews/Prices)"
- "Best 30-Inch Professional Gas Ranges (Reviews/Ratings/Prices)"

Sheinkopf didn't just stop with a smarter approach to the type of content he was producing. He also made content production a companywide policy, going so far as to add mandatory content production into the employee handbook.

> Some people are bad writers, I get that. But the other good part of getting everyone to blog is, theoretically if everyone is blogging and really trying, they'll learn to get better. If you spend a month researching a topic, you're going to know what you're talking about on that subject. And if you know what you're talking about, you should be able to explain it to others.

Even though Sheinkopf made it company policy that everyone in the organization had to help in producing content, whether researching and writing articles, helping draft new ideas, or participating in video shoots, Sheinkopf himself has written a majority of Yale Appliance's content, contributing more than 1,600 of his own articles.

> People would often question why the CEO of a company was working so hard on producing content when there were over 140 employees that could have been handling it. I actually started to feel bad about it.
>
> But then I was talking with Ann Handley [author of *Everybody Writes* and *Content Rules*] and she told me what I was doing was a good thing. She said, "You're in business development." And I thought, "Yeah, that's my real job. I'm in business development."
>
> Some of my articles have now been read 10 to 20 thousand times, and my top article has been read over 800,000 times. I couldn't advertise for that. That's why I do it, because I'm in business development.

With their retargeted marketing efforts, Yale Appliance's website traffic, leads, customers, and revenue began to grow at an incredible rate, doubling nearly every year from 2011 until the present. In fact, at the time of this writing, their traffic averages more than 800,000 monthly visitors in 2019!

Yale Appliance Tackles the Tougher Questions

A big part of Yale's success is because of their steadfast commitment to writing articles that genuinely help consumers make the most well-informed purchasing decisions possible, even if it means riffling a few major manufacturers' feathers along the way.

If you want to read an article that manufacturers really hate, read my article on "The 5 Most Serviced/Least Reliable Appliance Brands." I take people through the whole process of what it's like to buy something, and what the problems they may encounter are.

We don't just sell appliances; we service appliances as well. And because we service appliances we have actual service data that we can pull from a database that tells us which brands, makes, and models end up needing the most services and repairs.

Think about that for a second.

How many business owners in the retail space would be willing to openly publish the good, the bad, and the ugly of the very brands and products they sell?

How many would admit when one had a very high service rate?

How many would be so bold as to be specific about the problems of that particular appliance?

Almost none.

But that's also why almost no one has experienced the extreme success of Yale Appliance. Simply put, they care only about becoming the most trusted source in the world for consumers when it comes to appliances. That's it, and they let the rest of the chips fall as they may.

For example, though Sheinkopf's commitment to transparency and honesty is adored by his customers, his articles don't always sit well with the manufacturers. On more than one occasion he has been threatened with legal action for his earnest reviews.

I've had brands threaten to sue me over claims I've made in articles, but I don't mind, because what I'm saying is the truth, and I have the data to back up my claims. So when I've been threatened by brands, I say, "OK, well, I guess we'll have to give you all of our documentation, but we want the same from you. We want your records, too." And as long as we're right, nobody wants to do that.

Even though Sheinkopf's articles may appear to be hard-hitting to some of the major appliance brands, he sees his articles as a potential wake-up call to the manufacturers to improve their products.

I just report what I see. It's not up to me to make their products. They should take the advice of what's wrong with it and build it back up so it doesn't break. Threatening to sue me? It's the dumbest mentality. You shouldn't shoot the messenger for delivering the message that other people are saying, too. You can't fault me for saying it. They should take the advice and make improvements to their product. I'm not going to trash them with imaginary stuff. That would be irresponsible. What I'm trying to sell is truth and honesty.

Yale Appliance's Success with Inbound Marketing

Publishing articles based on truth, honesty, and transparency about appliances has served Yale Appliance very well. Today, Yale Appliance spends almost no money on advertising and focuses all of its marketing efforts into its website, blog, and learning center. And, says Sheinkopf, the results have been amazing.

> You want to talk ROI? What is my ROI? My investment is simple—it's my time, it's my team's time.
>
> You put our salaries together and it's still way under what we could have spent for advertising, and we still would have needed someone to maintain that anyway. Just by looking at a customer's email address (that was attracted through our content marketing efforts) and connecting it to a purchase, we can say that it's at least *$10 million in sales a year*. And that's with *zero advertising*.

When others tell Sheinkopf that traditional advertising really does work, he has a few strong words on the subject.

> People have always quoted me as "anti-outbound," but I'm not that at all. If you're getting a return on your investment through radio, home-shows, television ads, then all the more power to you.
>
> Typically, when people say advertising works I say, "How do you measure it?" They say, "It's impossible to measure." Then how do you know it works?
>
> People don't want advertising. They want to contact you when *they're* ready to contact you. There's a difference between me telling you I'm great and somebody reading something and saying, "Wow, that was great." If you, the customer, says it, there's a better shot at me earning your business.

If I [were] to advertise saying "Shop at Yale because we have a sale" by buying an audience of 500,000, how many people in that audience are actually in the market to buy something?

And of those people, how many are actually listening and not changing the channel or fast-forwarding? You're paying $500,000 for 20 people ... **maybe**. Where's the ROI on that? It's not measurable.

Inbound, assuming you use the right tools, is measurable, and we're going to stick with what works, and what we can measure.

And boy, has it worked for Sheinkopf.

Since embracing They Ask, You Answer, he now has three stores instead of one, sales are up from $37 million to over $120 million annually, and even his margins are up 5 percent—in a brutal industry where razor-thin margins are the name of the game for so many.

To say Sheinkopf's results have been stunning would be an understatement.

By simply obsessing over customer questions and being willing to answer them better than anyone else in their space, they've climbed to the top of their industry.

Once again, a digital David beats Goliath.

23

The Competition

Now that we've discussed the power of The Big 5 in detail, the question, of course, is whether or not your company is willing to address this new way of thinking.

Sadly, despite the overwhelming evidence that has been shared in this book, most people and organizations will not take such a transparent, buyer-centric approach to their sales and marketing efforts.

The question is, *"Why?"*

Why won't more organizations follow this incredibly simple model of They Ask, You Answer when it's so very obvious that buyers and consumers expect to have this information?

As I've consulted with so many businesses and brands around the world during the past eight years, I've discovered there are three fundamental factors that dictate whether businesses are willing to be world-class listeners and teachers versus taking the opposite approach—a more traditional, closed-minded company-centric model—to growing their businesses.

I call these three factors the "Triangle of Influence":

- Competition
- Bad fits
- Customer

Imagine an upside-down triangle that has three distinct sections, as shown in Figure 23.1. Each section represents a group that affects how willing a company is to address a particular subject in their sales and marketing process—especially online.

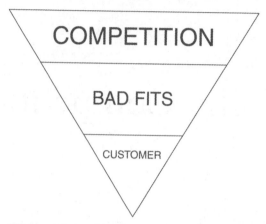

Figure 23.1   The Triangle of Influence

The top section is the largest and most influential factor influencing a company's reluctance to address the major questions, problems, and needs of prospective customers. The middle section is less influential than the top section, and the bottom section is the least influential of all.

Based on what we've discussed so far in this book, which do you think is the main group (the top section of the triangle) that affects whether or not a company is willing to address the questions—especially The Big 5—of their prospects and customers?

Before we discuss the three sections of the triangle, I am going to let you, the reader, guess where I am going with this. What would you guess is the most influential group of people determining what you will and will not talk about online and off?

If you guessed the competition, you are right.

In Chapter 10, when we talked about addressing cost and price on your website, you may have thought to yourself: *"I can't possibly do that because the competition will see what's written and use it against me with buyers."*

Then, in Chapter 13, we discussed problems and issues with your products and services and the importance of talking about these problems. Again, you likely said to yourself: *"If we openly talk about the pros and cons of our products and services, the competition will use it as a competitive advantage."*

In Chapter 17, we talked about the importance of comparing products and services (like fiberglass and concrete swimming pools), as well as the need to admit when you're not the best fit for a prospect.

Once again, you may be thinking: *"I can't possibly introduce them to alternative solutions to my products and services that my competitors are selling."*

And finally, in Chapter 19, we talked about addressing the competition directly, as we did with our "Who Are the Best Pool Builders in Richmond, Virginia (Reviews/Ratings)" article. With this one, the most controversial and unorthodox of all, you may have been thinking: *"I can't possibly talk about my competition on my site! If I do, the prospect will learn about the competition and instead of choosing me, the prospect will choose them."*

It is for these reasons that the competition is the most influential group affecting what most businesses will and will not address online today.

Think about that for a second.

The same group that has the greatest impact on businesses' willingness to discuss what their prospects and customers want to know is the very group they're competing against, and the one that is already taking some of their business. In many ways, it's a case of double jeopardy.

People ask me all the time, *"Marcus, if I start doing this—being honest and transparent and answering all these questions—what will happen if the competition sees what I'm doing and they do it, too?"*

Well, let me give you an example of how this works. Before I started my digital marketing agency and before I started speaking to so many groups and conferences, I was speaking to the swimming pool industry on this subject.

So believe it or not, everything that you have read in this book up to this point I have taught to pool companies all over the country in workshops at annual industry conferences. Even more interesting, many of the attendees of these workshops were the very companies I was competing with on a daily basis at River Pool and Spas in Virginia.

I once did the math and concluded that I had taught the principles you've been reading in this book to well over one thousand swimming pool companies.

Based on this fact, how many of these companies do you suppose followed the principles of They Ask, You Answer even half as well as we did at River Pools and Spas?

The answer? One or two, maybe.

This is an example of the saying that you can lead a horse to water but you cannot make it drink.

Well over 90 percent of the time, even though they've been taught or shown how to do it, businesses won't embrace They Ask, You Answer. It makes me sad to say it, but it's true. They have the knowledge, but they won't use it for themselves.

Why not? The reason is threefold:

- They're thinking like business owners, not teachers. Teachers see the world differently. That's just a fact.
- They come from a scarcity mentality and don't believe there's room on top for everybody.
- They are still holding on to the idea that they're "different."

In my case, I wasn't afraid my competitors would use the They Ask, You Answer principles; I was afraid they *wouldn't* use them.

So I taught the entire swimming pool industry. I wanted to help these companies despite the fact that they were competing for some of my own customers. As far as I was concerned, truth is truth, and it wasn't mine to keep.

Furthermore, to me at least, it was just a matter of common sense. And in this case, common sense told me that giving people what they want, as honestly and transparently as possible, was the best way to do business, regardless of its *supposed* ramifications.

The Bad Fits

The second most influential group that dictates our communication and ability to teach as businesses online and off is more subtle. Often, we don't even realize that this group has a major impact on things.

Let me give you a specific example of this influential group. If I say to you, "You should address the subject of pricing and costs on your site," a natural response, without knowing the benefits we've discussed, would be, *"Well, Marcus, if I address the subject of pricing and costs on my site, I will scare customers away."*

Let's think about this statement.

"I will scare customers away."

But are they even customers at all? No.

Look at it like this: If your products and services start at $50,000, and that person has a true budget of $20,000, do you think he is magically going to come up with an extra $30,000 for your products and/or services?

In most cases, the answer is no. Instead of scaring the person, you're going to educate him, which brings relief and saves time for all parties involved.

We are talking about being honest enough to allow—that's right, *allow*—the prospective customers to discover on their own that they are a bad fit for *you*.

If you've been in business for any length of time, you know as well as I do that not everybody is a good fit for you. In fact, the most successful companies have a very clear understanding of the fact they aren't a good fit for everyone and therefore embrace this reality instead of resisting it.

The moment a business thinks it wants to work with everyone is the moment that business starts to become very, very unhappy. Conversely, one of the happiest moments in the life of any business is the moment that they realize what they are *not*, and who they are *not* a good fit for.

In fact, if you think about all the "bad customers" you've had while in business who ended up not being a good fit for you, there's a very good chance that you realized, before they became customers, that your gut was telling you, *"This person or company is not a good fit for us."*

Ignoring that impression, you still did business with them. And the reason was that you needed the cash flow at the time. (We've all been there.)

Then, when things between you and the customer deteriorated, stress mounted, and you stopped enjoying working with them, you got out of bed in extreme frustration and said to yourself, *"The money isn't worth it!"*

Therefore, even though it's important for a business to know what they are, the happiest businesses in the world have a deep understanding of what they are *not*.

That's right—the second most influential group that dictates what we do and do not talk about is made up of the bad fits. We allow those people, *who will never become our customers,* to dictate our ability to listen, communicate, teach, and help.

And it's a tragedy.

The Customer

The only group that we *should* allow to dictate what we as businesses do and do not communicate to our customers (both online and off) is also the *least* influential group: the actual customer. Yes, the people who are giving us their trust, money, and even referrals are the ones we often overlook and ignore.

As you look at the triangle in Figure 23.1, tell me, what's wrong with the diagram? The natural reaction would be to say, *"Marcus, it should be flipped upside down."*

When I first started teaching these principles, that's what I thought as well. Then I realized I was completely wrong. There should only be one group inside the triangle: the actual customer, as represented in Figure 23.2.

When all is said and done, they are the only ones who truly matter.

They are the ones who will keep your lights on.

They are the ones who will allow you to live in financial peace.

And no one else.

Until the day your competition is paying your mortgage, and those bad fits who will never become your customers are funding your payroll, I urge you to consider focusing on the only group that truly matters.

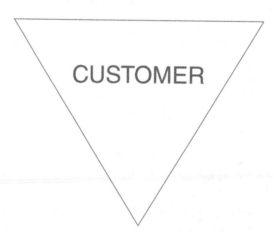

Figure 23.2 The Actual Customer

24

How They Ask, You Answer Saved River Pools and Spas

At this point, you may be wondering what the final impact of They Ask, You Answer was on River Pools and Spas.

As mentioned at the beginning of the book, in March 2009 we at River Pools and Spas were getting ready to lose our business. After learning about inbound and content marketing, we embraced what we called They Ask, You Answer and brainstormed every single question we had ever been asked by a prospect or customer. Night after night, after having heard multiple questions during the day from prospects, I (with the help of my business partners) wrote articles and produced videos addressing these questions.

When we first started this process, we were receiving about 2,000 visitors a month, and most of that traffic was coming from pay-per-click traffic on Google. We were spending about $500 every two days, and the money had finally run out.

But within three months of beginning to generate content, our site's organic (free) traffic began to double. Then, month after month, it just kept getting better.

Although 2009 was our toughest financial year as a company, we managed to survive. Our focus on content and great teaching was just enough to scratch and claw our way to at least keeping the lights on.

By 2010, I could see the work was starting to pay off. Our traffic and leads had exploded. The sales began to pour in.

Today, River Pools and Spas has thousands and thousands of inbound links coming from other sites—even though we never attempted a "link-building" campaign to increase these numbers. This all happened simply because other sites and companies thought our content was useful and helpful enough to link to.

In 2014, our traffic peaked in the month of July with 350,000 visitors to our site.

In July 2015, it reached more than 500,000 visitors.

And in 2016, we cross the 600,000-visitor threshold.

Now, River Pools and Spas is the most trafficked swimming pool website *in the world.*

Not only that, but in 2015, because of the tremendous growth, it was a natural progression for us to begin the manufacturing process as well.

Now, instead of being just a small installer of fiberglass swimming pools, we are in the process of developing a base of dealers throughout the United States. Based on where we are today, my guess is that, within the next five to seven years, we will become the largest manufacturer of fiberglass swimming pools in the world.

In conjunction with this, I'll share a couple of other statistics about River Pools and Spas that may astound you. In 2007, when home values were inflated and anybody could get credit to buy a swimming pool, we did about $4 million in business. In order to do $4 million in business, we had to spend about $250,000 on our advertising and marketing efforts.

In contrast, if you fast-forward to 2014—a time when most swimming pool builders were still dramatically down from the pre-recession time period—we did about $5.5 million in business and spent roughly $20,000 on advertising and marketing.

By 2018, revenue exceeded $8 million.

So I can only laugh when people ask me, *"Marcus, what will be our return on investment if we follow the principles of They Ask, You Answer?"*

I am someone who has been there and done everything I'm sharing with you. Everything you have read up to this point in the book saved our company and helped make it what it is today.

Now, when I look back at the crash of 2008, I do it with an incredible sense of gratitude. Those low moments forced me to look outside of myself and the industry, and forced us, as a company, to do things as they had never been done in the swimming pool space.

What is crazy about all of this is that we are just a small swimming pool installation company in Virginia with about 60 employees, and yet we're dictating the education of swimming pool shoppers all over the world.

Every day at River Pools, we receive emails from people all over the globe who want us to install their swimming pools.

Even though I am no longer in the swimming pool industry full-time, I still receive these emails from places as far removed from Virginia as Australia, Europe, and the Virgin Islands. These emails often say something along these lines: *"Marcus, we just don't trust our swimming pool contractor. Would you come out and oversee our swimming pool installation?"*

Long before I became "Marcus the Sales and Marketing Guy," I was turning down these requests, even though people were willing to pay me lots of money just to go out and oversee their swimming pool installation.

Why would I say no if I was being offered so much money to simply be an overseer? Well, I'll let you in on a little secret: *I can't install a pool.* I can't even turn on our excavator at River Pools. I am probably the worst pool builder in the world, and believe me, I'm the last person you want to see installing a swimming pool in your backyard.

But what I can do is look at how things are done with our installers (the real experts), ask them about what they're doing, and explain it in a way so that the average person understands how it is done. Because I can distill the facts into simple-to-understand words that pool shoppers find helpful, they naturally think I am one of the foremost authorities in the world.

Someone once told me, *"It's dumb not to dumb it down."*

At the time, I had no idea how right they were.

Since that moment, I've seen again and again how, when it comes to great marketing and communication, the moment a business or brand tries to sound smart is generally the moment they start to look stupid.

But when you don't try to sound smart, and instead try to have open communication with your listener, that's when the magic happens. For me, this is my singular goal and obsession as a professional speaker, marketer, and communicator.

My point to you is this: Think like a teacher. Obsess not just over the questions, but the way you answer them. This approach will make all the difference.

PART

II

The Impact of They Ask, You Answer on Sales Teams

Up to this point in the book, much of what we have discussed has to do with the marketing side of They Ask, You Answer. But when all is said and done, being found on Google and increasing traffic, leads, and trust is just one of the many benefits of creating a company culture of obsessive listening and teaching.

In fact, the biggest benefit to this type of business philosophy has much more to do with selling than with anything else. At the end of the day—regardless of the increased traffic and leads great content produces—if you're not generating new business, the end result is a failure.

As businesses, we *must* generate a profit.

Having personally looked over the cliff called "bankruptcy," I can attest to the truthfulness of this statement.

In this part of the book, we analyze how the principles found in They Ask, You Answer, when applied properly, go well beyond your marketing department, permeating your entire sales team and organization.

We show you their impact on sales teams, their culture, their ability to close, and exactly how you can better use content to dramatically increase your sales numbers.

25

How Great Content Is a Total Game-Changer for Sales Teams

Let's assume for a minute that you're committed to making content marketing and the principles of They Ask, You Answer work within your organization.

In order to make this happen, not only do the leadership and marketing teams have to be aligned in their vision, but the sales team must immediately get involved in the process.

That means they must understand the *what*, *how*, and *why* of this important business strategy. Additionally, they must realize that there are multiple reasons why embracing this way of selling will affect not just the organization, but each salesperson individually as well.

Listed next are seven benefits that sales teams need to understand will occur if they're properly integrating They Ask, You Answer into the sales process.

The 7 Major Benefits of Sales Teams Embracing They Ask, You Answer

1. Producing Content Forces Us to Understand the Buyers and the Way They Think

If you're going to be good at content marketing as an organization, you'd better be *great* at understanding exactly what prospects and customers are saying, thinking, feeling, and searching. You must know their pains, worries, issues, and desires. Simply put, you must be dialed in.

In the marketing space, one might call this a "buyer persona." But regardless of what it's called, many organizations and sales teams never quite reach a point at which they are completely in tune with the way their customers and prospects think before, during, and after the buying process.

But when companies are forced to think about these things while they're attempting to produce educational and helpful content aligned to each phase of the buyer's journey, the ability for the sales team to put themselves in the shoes of their prospects and customers will never be higher.

In sales, empathy is everything. When salespeople don't have it, they generally aren't very successful. And when they don't have it with their content, it generally doesn't work either.

2. Producing Content Is a Magical Practice for Sales Messaging

The best sales professionals have not only heard most questions a prospect could ask, but they tend to answer them the same way each time. Furthermore, their answers are clearly stated and communicated in such a way that the prospect understands and their concerns have been resolved.

This type of effective communication is needed for every great sales pro, but it doesn't happen immediately, and it certainly takes practice. For this reason content marketing can be very powerful. It helps the sales pros (as they produce the content) learn how to better answer questions, explain in an intelligible way, and achieve the desired results.

Here at IMPACT, we've heard time and time again how our clients improved overall sales communication *after* their sales team became involved in the content production process. (Don't worry, we will talk more about the content production process later in the book.)

3. Company Content Acts as the Primary Guide for All Training, Messaging, Etc.

Even though sales departments have always been considered the financial heartbeat of most organizations, and even though their ability to have uniformity in what they communicate and teach to clients has always been extremely important, most companies have never taken the time to write out their "sales doctrine" for all employees and sales team members.

As you might imagine, this is where content marketing and They Ask, You Answer come into play. Through in-house articles, videos, and so on, current and future employees will have a database of training content that will help them to learn the company doctrines and philosophies faster and more effectively, affecting the human resources side of the organization for years to come.

4. Assignment Selling

It's a crying shame just how silo-driven many organizations are. Marketing sticks with marketing, and sales sticks with sales. But the most successful companies understand that the two should be aligned, and sales should use the content produced by marketing throughout the sales process. The concept of using content intentionally to educate consumers and push them further down (or out of) the sales funnel is what we at IMPACT call "assignment selling."

We discuss assignment selling in more detail later in Chapter 27.

5. Sales Teams Can Learn What Prospects and Customers Truly Care About Before They Enter the Sales Funnel

With the plethora of advanced analytics and other tools available to sales teams today, there is absolutely no reason not to take advantage of deeper lead intelligence. For example, assuming a lead has filled out a contact form on your website, advanced analytics allow you to see every page that person has viewed on the site. It allows you to know how many times he or she has visited. It can also notify you every time that person returns to the website in the future.

By looking at these analytics, a sales professional can start to piece together the "story" of the prospect long before the initial contact or phone conversation. This knowledge can be an absolute game-changer for a sales team.

6. *With Content, a Relationship of Trust Can Be Built with the Salesperson (and Company) Long Before the First Sales Meeting*

Every salesperson wants better leads. They also want to go on better sales calls. Unfortunately, many sales calls and presentations have to be focused—at least for the first part of the meeting—on building trust (instead of the "selling" part). But with the digital consumer of today, it's possible to build that trust (much more, in fact, than in a 20-minute conversation) long before the initial sales meeting.

This allows a sales pro to do what they do best—*sell*.

7. *Great Content Means More Trust, More Trust Means Shorter Sales Cycles, and Shorter Sales Cycles Mean Happier Sales Teams*

Not only do all sales pros want more (good) leads, but they also want more *time*. Time to spend on more qualified opportunities. Time to spend with their families and loved ones. Time to do those things they enjoy most.

Fact is, great teaching (They Ask, You Answer) can be the ultimate "time giver" to a sales department.

In the following chapters, you'll see some astounding examples of how using content in the sales process can not only save time, but have a tremendous impact on sales cycles and closing rates in general.

This is the essence of understanding just how much impact content marketing can have on a sales team and organization. Once companies start to understand the benefits of engaging their sales teams in the content production process, magic will assuredly happen.

26 | A Dramatic Discovery

Let me start by asking you a very important question: *On average, how many pages of your website do you think someone would be willing to read before they do business with you?*

This is a question I've asked audiences all over the world. And in every industry and every country, I get pretty much the same answer: *"Two or three pages."*

Let's look at that figure. How long do you suppose it would take someone to read two or three pages of your site?

Conservatively, let's assume the length of time is about five minutes.

What you're really saying when you say that you can only envision a prospective customer reading (on average) two or three pages of your site is this: *"Marcus, doing business with us is worth about five minutes of someone's time."*

But do you really think the process of deciding to do business with you is worth *only* five minutes of someone's time? ***I'd certainly hope this isn't the case.***

As businesses, we grossly *underestimate* people's willingness to consume information in their quest to become informed and comfortable with a buying decision. To help you understand this point further, let me tell you about a dramatic discovery I made in 2012 related to my swimming pool company—one that has since affected many, many other businesses with its universal effectiveness.

At the beginning of 2012, I was comparing two groups of people who had filled out the "I want to get a quote" form on my swimming pool website.

By filling out the form, both groups of people had shown they'd gained enough trust to potentially want to do business with us. But here was the difference between the two:

- The first group filled out a form but did *not* buy from us.
- The second group filled out a form and *did* buy from us.

As I was looking at these two groups of people, I kept asking myself again and again: *"What was the differentiator? What makes some buy but others not buy? What was the key indicator that would lead someone to say 'Yes'?"*

As I was using HubSpot (more about them later) to look at the analytics on our site, I discovered something interesting about the number 30 related to the second group—the one that had bought swimming pools from us.

Can you guess what the number 30 represented?

If you guessed "total pages viewed," you hit the nail on the head.

Now you may be thinking, *"Wow, 30 pages is a lot!"*

That's certainly what I thought when I discovered this anomaly. And it became even more interesting as we explored those numbers further. We discovered that if someone read 30 or more pages of the website before the initial sales appointment, *they would buy from us 80 percent of the time.*

By contrast, if they didn't read 30 or more pages, *the average closing rate in terms of appointment-to-sale was only 25 percent.*

This was a phenomenal discovery. For me, in that moment, my relationship with this thing we call "content" reached a much deeper understanding and appreciation. It also made me rethink our entire sales process.

Such a stat begs the following questions: *What is happening over the course of a prospect reading 30 pages that caused such a dramatic increase in terms of their closing rates? And why is there such a big difference between the prospects who didn't read 30 pages of our site and those who did?*

You have to look at it like this:

- Every time someone consumes a piece of your content (video, article, podcast, and so on), the trust factor continues to rise. Throughout the process, they are essentially "self-qualifying."
- Every piece of content that someone reads or watches becomes the equivalent of another meeting—or "date"—with that person.
- If you go on enough dates with someone, eventually, you'll get "married."

- Or you will break up.
- One way or another, over the course of 30 dates, you're going to clearly discover whether or not you're a good fit, and whether you want to continue forward with each other. The same thing is true with great content.

That being said, let's say that you found out that all you had to do was get a prospect to consume 30 pieces of your content (articles, videos, and so on) and he or she would buy from you 80 percent of the time. If that were true, what would you do differently? How would you handle that information? And how would that change your sales numbers?

The answer to these questions is what comes next—*assignment selling*.

27 | Assignment Selling

Often, when businesses embrace content marketing and They Ask, You Answer, the tendency is to think: *"OK, I'm just going to post this on my site and great things are going to happen!"*

Unfortunately, publishing content on your site simply is not enough. You can't just passively post content on your website or social media channels and expect it to work its magic. You must find ways to help your prospects and customers read and view your content if you're going to move the needle. Furthermore, you can't be passive about this, and you can't just leave it up to chance.

The process of actively using your content in the sales process is what I've dubbed "assignment selling."

To help you catch the vision that is assignment selling, we'll again use swimming pools as an example. But before we go any further, let me explain what I'm talking about when I use the phrase "assignment selling."

I define assignment selling as:

> The process of intentionally using information:
> - Which you have created via text, video, or audio.
> - That is educational about your products and/or services.
> - With the purpose of resolving the major concerns and questions of prospects so they are dramatically more prepared for a sales appointment—or multiple sales appointments.

I reference assignment selling as something necessary to do before and during the sales process.

An Example of Assignment Selling in Action

As you read the following, I don't want you to think you have to apply this to your business *in the exact same way* that I show here. The key is the way information or content is used to help your prospects either move down the sales funnel and advance or become disqualified because they discover they're not a good fit for you.

Here is how it works:

It used to be that someone would call my swimming pool company and say something like, *"Hey, Marcus, I'm checking out your website and I think I'd like to get a quote for a swimming pool. Can you come out to my house this Friday and give me a quote?"*

After asking them a couple of qualifying questions, I would say, "Sure, I'll be right out." I did that because that's what I thought salespeople were supposed to do. If I was asked to go out and sell, I wanted to immediately go out and sell. At that time, I didn't know any better.

This occurred because I wasn't truly thinking about the readiness of the prospect. I wasn't asking myself, *"Well, wait a minute here. How much does this person really understand about the world of swimming pools?"*

When I responded immediately to their request for a swimming pool quote, I had no way of knowing how educated they were with respect to buying a swimming pool. A person might be very informed and educated regarding our products and services, or might be totally ignorant and aloof. Really, I knew nothing about my prospects and customers, and for all I knew, they knew absolutely nothing about what I was trying to sell them.

But I was not alone in my struggles. Many sales professionals are experiencing this very thing to some degree or another.

How does one overcome this ignorance on the part of potential buyers? How does a sales professional take a prospect from "uninformed" to "*extremely* educated?"

At River Pools, we changed our entire sales conversations, starting with the first call. This is how it now sounded:

POOL SHOPPER: Hey Marcus, I've been checking out your site and I think I'd like to get a quote for a swimming pool. Can you come out to my house this Friday and give me a quote?

ME: Of course, I would love to come out to your house this Friday and give you a quote. However, you're getting ready to spend a lot of money on a swimming pool, and I know you don't want to make any mistakes with a project of this magnitude. So, to ensure you don't make any mistakes, we're going to help you become well educated.

To do this, I'm going to send you an email. In this email, you're going to see two main things. First, you're going to see a video of a fiberglass swimming pool installation. This will let you know how the swimming pool is going to show up to your house; it will show you the excavation and shell going in the ground; and it will also allow you to see the final grade-work and cleanup. In other words, you'll observe the whole process so that, when I come out to your house, you won't have to ask me, "Marcus, what does this process look like?" You will already know. That will save us both a lot of time.

The second thing I'm going to do is attach an ebook to this email, which is essentially a buying guide. You will find this information extremely helpful as well, as it will answer many of the questions you have right now.

For example, it will address questions about what would be the best cover for your swimming pool: solid, mesh, or maybe even an automatic cover. The guide will also go over subjects like pool heaters and address questions of whether gas or electric is better, or whether you even need a heater at all.

It's a little bit long—*about 30 pages*—but I promise you, it will be well worth your time.

Then I close by saying, *"So Mr./Mrs. Jones, would you take the time to review this ebook before our appointment on Friday?"*

Having had this exact conversation with hundreds of swimming pool shoppers, I can tell you that 90 percent of the time, the simple response is, *"Sure."*

At this point in the conversation, I would respond by saying, *"That's great. Friday morning, I will give you a call just to confirm our appointment as well as make sure you took the time to do those two things."*

The Special Rights of the Teacher

Asking prospects to do this type of "homework" beforehand, and then letting them know you'll confirm whether they did said homework or not, sounds audacious.

And you're right. It is bold. It is audacious.

But it's also incredibly effective.

The reason we have such an approach to selling is because our focus on teaching gives us the right to ask for commitments from prospects.

First, in this case, I have taken the time to give prospects tremendous value by producing a video that is going to walk them through the process of buying a fiberglass swimming pool. Second, we've created a guide that is going to answer the majority of their other pool-related questions. There is an extreme amount of value in producing this content for them. And because I've done this, I've earned the right to ask more of the prospect, which, in this case, is to review the video and ebook.

But I couldn't, for example, say, *"I found a book all about buying fiberglass swimming pools written by a guy in California, and I want you to read it before we meet."*

First, the book I would be asking the prospect to read would not be filled with my words, and I would not have therefore earned the right—nor authority—to ask the prospect to read the book (or do the homework).

Second, by producing content in the form of text or video and posting that content on your site and other platforms, you take on the role of teacher. And the moment your prospects see you more as a teacher versus a salesperson, the amount of respect they have for you dramatically escalates.

Remember: The rights of a teacher are greater than those of the person who does not teach.

You may be asking yourself: *"What happens if they say, 'You know, Marcus, it's great that you put together this ebook, but I won't have time to read it before Friday. Just come on out and give me a quote.'?"*

How do you respond to that? Before you read the response, keep in mind here what I stated at the beginning of this section: *The way we are able to sell at River Pools and Spas may be different from the way you sell.*

At River Pools, we can be a little pickier with our clients. Because we get a massive number of leads every day, we can qualify harder than other companies based on what we sell, who we sell to, and how much we have to sell in order to be successful.

That being said, we should all be looking for ways to help our prospects become more educated before we talk with them the first time, and then we should continue to educate them throughout the sales process.

Here is our response at River Pools when someone says they don't have enough time:

Mr./Mrs. Jones, I appreciate the fact that you don't have the time to review this content, but here's the thing—over the years, we have found that when our customers are very informed and take the time to review the things I am sending to you, we have a wonderful experience when we meet with them in their homes.

In other words, it makes for a much more productive meeting and seriously eliminates buying mistakes on their part. This way, the customer is happy, and we are happy.

But when they don't do these things, the experience is not nearly as good nor productive. So, Mr./Mrs. Jones, if you don't have time to become informed and educated about these things, then we are probably not the best fit for you.

As you read this, you may be thinking, *"Do you actually tell them they're probably not the best fit for you?"*

Yes, we do. And I can tell you exactly how they're going to react because I've heard such a response many times. In fact, everything you're reading about assignment selling and using content as a sales tool has been vetted and experimented with hundreds of times at River Pools. Not only that, but this is exactly how we do things at IMPACT with our clients, giving us the opportunity to apply these exact same principles to large and small businesses and brands all over the world.

Remember, the principle of making sure we are dealing with educated prospects and customers essentially does not change from business to business, regardless of what you sell.

Now back to Mr./Mrs. Jones's reaction upon me telling them that if they don't want to become a bit more educated, then they're probably not the best fit for my business. Almost all prospects have responded in one of two ways:

- **The first response sounds like this:** "OK, Marcus, fine. I will read your ebook and watch your video." And at that point I say, "Well, that's wonderful! Friday morning, I will call you just to confirm you've done those things."
- **The second response sounds like this:** "Forget you! I don't need you to come out to my house and I don't need you to sell me a swimming pool. I'll go somewhere else!"

When this happens, your response as a business should be one of gratitude, because you now know they're clearly not a good fit.

Here is the core principle we are really discussing:

If becoming educated with respect to your products and services is not a variable in a prospect's buying decision, it almost always means that person is basing a decision on what to buy solely on price. Unless your business model is one of being the lowest-priced option every time, *the prospect is very likely not a good fit for you.*

What Homework Can Tell Us About a Prospect

"Marcus, what happens if you call prospects on Friday morning to ask whether they did their homework and they say, 'Well, no, I haven't done it, but I still want you to come out and give me a quote.' What do you do then?"

That's a very good question, and that situation has come up many times as well.

When I first started this process, and a prospect would say, "I am so sorry, I got busy. But I still want you to come out and give me a quote," the salesman in me would think: *"Well, they didn't take the time to do it, but I guess I can still go out there."*

I tracked those sales appointments over the course of six months, and I was shocked at the results. Guess how many of the prospects who failed to do their homework but said, "Come out anyway and give me a quote" turned into customers?

If you guessed fewer than 5 percent, you are correct.

This goes back to my point:

- Homework (education) can tell us a lot about the prospect.
- When people don't take the time to become well educated, they are most likely making their decision based solely on price, which generally means they're not the best fit.
- When it comes to success in business, the difference between happiness and frustration comes down to knowing who is, and who is not, a good fit for your organization.

28

How One Remarkable Couple Changed My Perspective on the Power of Content to Sell

Now that we've established *how* to do assignment selling, let's revisit one of the first questions we asked in this section: *On average, how many pages of your website would a potential client or customer be willing to read?*

The following story is an example of what is possible. It's also, in many ways, going to sound unbelievable, but trust me when I say it's absolutely true.

I'm giving you an example of a customer experience I had that really changed my perspective in terms of the way teaching can affect the sales process, as well as the willingness of shoppers to consume information in order to become comfortable with a buying decision.

Around 2012, when I was still a pool guy, I was up late one night using HubSpot to look over the leads that had come in to my swimming pool website that day, and one of the leads was from a man named "Mr. G." I saw that he had come to the site because he was searching on Yahoo! for the phrase "cost of a fiberglass swimming pool."

But once he got to the website, something very interesting happened: *He viewed 374 pages!*

I know what was going through my mind when I saw this, and it's probably the same thing that's going through your mind. Right now, you're probably thinking: *"What in the world??!"*

There are a lot of assumptions you can make when you see that someone has viewed that amount of website content: *"My goodness! This man has way too much time on his hands!"*

Or *"Geez, he must be a competitor!"*

Or *"Maybe he has some sort of rare form of OCD, where he can't get enough information about swimming pools."*

In any case, I was very perplexed—and almost stunned—to learn just how much of our website content this individual had read.

But this isn't all—the story gets much more interesting.

The same night that I discovered that Mr. G had read 374 pages of our site, I was looking through the leads that came in when I noticed a lead from a lady named (Mrs.) G. It was easy to put two and two together and realize that Mr. G had a wife, who was also researching swimming pools.

What made this even funnier was that she had found us because she had been searching on Yahoo! and typed in "Richmond, Virginia, swimming pools."

On top of that, she had read more than *140 pages* of the website herself.

Now, if you take these two individuals combined, *this couple had read more than 500 pages of our site.*

More than 500 pages ... *about fiberglass swimming pools.*

The next day, I called Mr. G. He acted as though he had known me for years, and quickly agreed to have me out to his house for a sales appointment.

What do you suppose that sales appointment was like?

I will tell you. I walked into the house, and Mr. G was standing in his living room with a spreadsheet in his hands. On one side of the sheet was a model of the swimming pool that he was planning to buy, and on the other side of the sheet he had listed every option and accessory he was buying to go with the pool.

Of course, all he needed from me was one little thing: ***the price***.

I walked out of that appointment 45 minutes later with a $5,000 deposit and a signed contract in my hands. As I drove away from the home, I started to laugh, as a thought occurred to me: *"How much selling had I actually done that day?"*

None. The Gs weren't just 70 percent decided when I got there; they were more in the range of 99.9 percent decided that they were going to use our company.

Frankly, my only job on that day was: "Don't screw this one up, pool guy."

So I laughed.

It turns out that Mr. G was not a freak, not a competitor, and not retired. Rather, he was a surgeon. But he was also a consumer—a consumer who, along with his wife, wanted to feel comfortable with a buying decision.

In fact, if you think about how you buy things and how much research you do when you're serious about what you're buying, you'll see that you are likely grossly underestimating people's willingness to become comfortable with their buying decisions through the power of great, helpful information.

My appointment with the Gs was one of the last ones I went on as a pool guy. It was also easily one of the most powerful and memorable, because it taught me a clear lesson, one that I've seen time and time again, in multiple industries and businesses, all over the world:

Content—assuming it is honest and transparent—is the greatest sales tool in the world today.

29 | Content Never Sleeps

"Content—assuming it is honest and transparent—is the greatest sales tool in the world today."

That may sound to you like too bold a statement. You may also believe, especially if you're clinging to the past, that it's simply not true. But let's look at it together for a moment.

I used to think I was really good at sales. In fact, I taught sales classes and achieved some very high-performance numbers for years. But as a human being, I am limited.

Content, on the other hand, is not.

Here are some truths about content, especially the content on your website, assuming it's done right:

- Content can teach 1,000; 100,000; or even 1,000,000 people at a time. Its scope and reach have no limits. A salesperson, for the most part, can "teach" only those he or she is speaking in front of.
- Content never sleeps. It can work for you 24 hours a day, seven days a week, 365 days a year. It doesn't ask for holidays off. It doesn't get sick. It simply keeps going.
- Content doesn't need a commission and never asks for a raise. It won't leave you for another company, and it will follow the rules and dictates you give it.
- A single piece of content can continue to work for you long after you've forgotten about it. (Heck, many of the articles we've discussed here for River Pools are several years old, yet they generate hundreds of thousands of dollars each year in revenue. Essentially, they are "evergreen.")

131

Let me share some other telling statistics with you.

For years as a swimming pool salesman, my life was a total grind, consisting of incredible amounts of travel combined with sitting in front of homeowners day in and day out. And considering the average sales appointment lasted two to three hours, combined with the fact that most appointments were more than two hours from my home, you can see why things were a little rough.

To add further perspective, in order to sell 75 swimming pools in 2007, I had to go on roughly 250 sales appointments—a 30 percent closing ratio. That year, I worked well over 60 hours every week. Most nights I didn't get home until after 10 or 11 p.m.

Time with my family was, for the most part, nonexistent.

I don't mention these things to give myself a pat on the back. I'm simply trying to set the stage to showcase the difference the principles in this book can make if you're willing to apply them to your business. I don't know about you, but having no life outside of driving and selling probably isn't the healthiest way to make a living nor to develop a powerful sales culture that's built to last within an organization.

Now let's fast-forward to the point at which I started the process of assignment selling and integrating content throughout the sales process.

In 2013, we sold 95 swimming pools. To sell those 95 pools, we went on *120 sales appointments—a closing rate of **79** percent.* When I share these statistics with other swimming pool companies, they do not believe we could ever sell that many swimming pools with that few appointments.

But here is the big key they are missing:

Guess how many pages, on average, those 95 customers in 2013 read?

No, the answer is not 30.

It's not 50.

It's not even 80.

The answer, if you can believe it, was 105.

That's right, 95 customers, on average, were willing to read 105 pages of our website before they bought a swimming pool from our company.

And today the numbers are trending even higher.

To this day, despite having seen this same phenomenon in other industries with our clients, I'm still blown away with the results, as they're truly an astounding look at consumer behavior in the digital age.

"How is that even possible?"

Well, if you had come to me 10 years ago and asked: *"Marcus, do you realize that swimming pool customers would be willing to read more than 100 pages of your website before they buy?"*

I would have looked at you, called you a fool, and then proceeded to tell you that you were crazy and didn't understand my buyer, my customer, or my industry.

And I would have been dead wrong.

The sad reality is that, as some of you are reading these pages, you may still think your industry and your business are different, and these principles don't apply to you. But I'm here to tell you that the principles are exactly the same.

Over the past few years, every client we have had at IMPACT who has initiated They Ask, You Answer and become prolific teachers on their websites has also discovered just how much content people (B2B and B2C) will view on their site before making a buying decision.

I'd like to make a few other points before closing this chapter.

I mentioned to you that we went on 120 sales calls to close 95 sales in 2013. Think about that in terms of the impact on our salespeople. Instead of having to go on 250 sales appointments, our salespeople—who are arguably less skilled than I was all those years—now go on fewer than half that number; yet they have dramatically higher closing rates than I ever had.

Let's do the math. Each sales appointment involves at least two hours driving each way plus two to three hours at the actual appointment. That means that each sales appointment involves a time expenditure of six to seven hours on average. So, if we go on 130 fewer appointments to achieve even better results, we have just saved more than 800 person-hours in a year.

What can one salesperson do with 800 additional hours in the year? The answers are obvious. He or she can:

- Spend a lot more time with qualified prospects and buyers.
- Spend more time networking and focusing on business development.
- And, most important, spend more time doing that which he or she loves—be it with family, friends, loved ones, hobbies, and so on. Frankly, that's what it's all about.

The moral of the story: It is not just about leads, traffic, and sales. It is not just about building your brand either. ***It is about giving your company, your staff, and your salespeople more time.***

For time is the one thing that can never be recovered. Once it's gone, it's gone, and you will never be able to get it back. (I can personally attest to this, as I'm sure you can as well.)

If you can give this incredible gift (of time) to your employees, then not only do employee morale and overall culture improve, but you are making a serious impact on the world in the process.

30

How to Use Assignment Selling to Avoid Common Pitfalls

Before we finish with assignment selling, I want to show you how you can use this sales strategy to avoid common sales pitfalls and mistakes.

Here's a very common sales scenario: A salesperson gives a prospect a proposal or a quote and a few days go by without hearing back from the prospect. As the days go by, the salesperson starts to get nervous and sends the prospect an email. That email usually sounds something like this:

Hello, Mr./Mrs. Jones,

We met a couple of days ago and I gave you a proposal. I'm just checking in to see if you have any questions. Don't hesitate to let me know.

Sincerely, Salesperson

That email might as well be called a "Please-don't-break-up-with-me" letter because it essentially sounds like we're saying:

Dear Mr./Mrs. Jones,

Do you still love me? Yes or no? **I sure hope you circled yes!**

Almost everyone writes that type of email when a prospect goes silent after receiving a proposal or quote. But it's completely ineffective.

It's at moments like this when it's easy to see the incredible power of assignment selling. Using the principles of assignment selling, your email would consist of the following:

Hello, Mr./Mrs. Jones,

We met a few days ago and I gave you a proposal. During our meeting, you mentioned a couple of questions and concerns you had. In order to further help you with these concerns, I've attached to this email a video and an article that specifically address each.

Please take a moment to give each a look, as I know they'll help you with this important decision.

And tomorrow I'll give you a call so we can discuss.

Sincerely, Salesperson

When we meet someone in a sales situation and give our pitch or proposal, we generally believe we have properly addressed the person's concerns, and in the moment, we may have. But often those same concerns will resurface after the prospect has some time to reflect on our sales conversation or proposal.

So rather than writing a "Please-don't-break-up-with-me" email, writing an email like the second one has two major benefits.

First, it will remind your prospects that they actually have nothing to worry about. You are offering the best solution to their problems. It reaffirms your expertise related to their particular concerns.

Second, it will force your prospects to respond in one of two ways:

They may respond with a simple "Thank you, this is great! It is exactly what I needed." When they respond in this manner, it is a clear sign that they are interested, and things are looking very positive in terms of your ability to do business with them.

On the other hand, they may respond by telling you they are not interested, and you are not a good fit for them. Knowing that you are going to contact them to ask about the homework you have now given them forces them to tell you the truth.

As we've already discussed in this book: Time is your greatest asset in business and in life, and a candid answer like "I'm not interested" or "Actually, we've decided to go a different direction" saves you precious time.

You may be thinking right now that your business could not apply assignment selling to its sales process. I am here to tell you this is absolutely not the case.

In fact, each of the most successful clients we have worked with here at IMPACT, whether smaller companies or larger brands, have adopted this principle of using content in their sales processes. Sure, it changes based on their product, service, buyer, sales cycle, and other factors, but the principle of using education to sell does not change.

31 | How to Use Assignment Selling to Determine Compatibility

I want to start this chapter by giving you a simple example that's close to home. Here at our digital sales and marketing agency, IMPACT, we also utilize an assignment selling process with our prospects. Keep in mind that our clients are other businesses, not consumers.

Because we have a very high number of leads coming into our system, we need to make sure that we're working with good fits and not with bad fits. We want to make sure we're dealing with informed and educated clients versus those who really have no clue as to what we are and the services we provide—people who haven't done any research whatsoever.

In our case at IMPACT, we have a set of content (in video and textual format) that completely explains to a prospect our core philosophies of They Ask, You Answer, as well as what makes us unique as an agency. After a quick call with a member of our sales team immediately after the lead comes in, any prospect or company who is going to move to the next phase of the sales process has to have reviewed this content.

Without their doing this, we know it will present so many issues (of misaligned philosophies) in the sales process that we simply do not continue.

You may be wondering how we introduce this content to the prospect. On the first call with a prospect, it sounds something like this:

> Mr. Jones, in order to make this process as productive as possible for your team, and in order to ensure you end up choosing the right agency to help your business succeed, it's critical you understand our overall approach to digital sales and marketing.
>
> Specifically, we follow a business philosophy called They Ask, You Answer—which is a radically more transparent communication style than most agencies preach. We also believe that this effort starts with sales, and your sales team—not with marketing.
>
> Finally, we believe in the power of learning to use the process in-house, rather than simply paying an agency to do it for you, without you ever learning to do it for yourselves.
>
> But to understand this further, I'm going to ask you to review two videos that will fully explain the what, how, and why behind our beliefs. By reviewing them with your team, you'll know whether we are, or are not, a good fit for your organization.
>
> Will you commit to reviewing these two videos with your team before our next call?

Let's talk about a couple of things you just read in that phone conversation that make it unique.

First, you'll notice how the communication is based on the principle that if the prospect does certain things, *he or she* will have a better experience. This is much more effective than saying, *"Hey, Mr./Mrs. Jones, I really don't know if you're worth my time. In order to tell whether you are, please read this."*

The second principle that you will notice is the principle of disarmament, which we discussed in an earlier chapter. Here is how we have used disarmament with our prospects:

- We have come right out and admitted that there is a chance that we will not be a good fit for them.
- We have allowed prospects to feel like they are in charge of identifying whether we are a good fit or not. But in reality, *we* are also identifying whether they are a good fit for us.

You may be thinking: *"Marcus, there is no way somebody is going to watch two videos with their team every time!"*

You're right. If they don't want to take the time to educate themselves as to whether or not we're a good fit, then they certainly won't make the time investment. But this simply means they weren't a good fit to begin with.

Look at it like this: If somebody takes the time to do this so they understand our thoughts, teachings, and philosophy on sales and marketing, and then we have a full sales call, the productivity of that sales conversation will be drastically higher than if no previous learning had over occurred.

That's the beauty of assignment selling.

Agencies like ours have, like many other industries, become commoditized. By ensuring our prospects are well informed, we can now decommodotize what we do and how we do it, ultimately making us very different, and much more attractive to the marketplace.

I want to reiterate that we've worked with companies of all shapes and sizes that have made assignment selling work for them in their own ways.

A few core principles remain consistent, namely:

- Every email sent out by your company's sales team is a teaching opportunity. So stop sending out emails—especially emails of the sales variety—that do not include content that teaches the prospect or customer. It doesn't make sense.
- If you are going to implement assignment selling and use content in your company's sales process, the sales team must be informed and be aware of the content that is being produced.

In the following chapter, we'll discuss this subject and the incredible need for sales and marketing departments to become completely aligned into one unit, without silos.

32

Case Study 4

How a Healthcare Startup Became the Thought Leaders of an Entirely New Industry

Life as a startup isn't easy.

It's even more difficult when you're competing against some of the biggest brands in the world. But that's the beauty of the internet. It's the great equalizer. As previously mentioned, those companies willing to do things differently and clear their own paths can often do exceptional things.

Such has been the case with Health Catalyst.

About Health Catalyst

Health Catalyst is unique in that it came into an industry that was still in its infancy—healthcare analytics. Founded in 2010, Health Catalyst is a data warehousing, analytics, and outcomes improvement company that provides infrastructure so that healthcare organizations (hospitals) can identify waste in their practices, allowing them to improve patient care and lower their overall costs.

In its new space, Health Catalyst quickly found that almost no one was answering industry questions online. Even though massive brands were starting to enter the space, no one was established as the industry's voice of trust.

Because of this, no real information existed online for interested searchers.

Health Catalyst recognized there was a huge informational void in their industry, and they set out to fill it. Unlike other businesses, Health Catalyst didn't have to fight to have their voice heard, because there were no other voices. Rather than push their way onto the stage, Health Catalyst built the stage.

Paul Horstmeier, Health Catalyst senior vice president and former Hewlett-Packard vice president, was brought on board in 2012 when the company was ready to scale its sales and marketing efforts. Most of Health Catalyst's marketing until that point had been through word-of-mouth referrals and press releases. Horstmeier was asked to start a marketing campaign nearly from scratch. Because he was a little rusty in heading a marketing department, Horstmeier started researching how companies were doing quality marketing.

> I decided I needed to get up to speed with what was the latest and greatest in marketing. I started reading and looking at the concept of content marketing. I don't remember how, but I came across Marcus Sheridan's ebook, *Inbound and Content Marketing Made Easy*, and his philosophy (They Ask, You Answer) fit with what I already believed, so we had him come out for a workshop a few months later.

The base principles of They Ask, You Answer harmonized with Horstmeier's own philosophy of creating a culture in his industry based on educating the marketplace, rather than building a brand that simply sold a product and services.

> I thought traditional marketing was dead. Most of the data that I had done in my research confirmed it. Only about 30 percent of people actually trust brands. So for the most part, you have to start from the perspective that nobody trusts what you're saying.

Horstmeier had no trouble convincing his partners that the direction Health Catalyst needed to move in was to focus on properly educating the marketplace. Before the initial workshop even kicked off, Health Catalyst already had top-to-bottom buy-in, a clear direction they wanted to take the company, and a new marketing team ready to carry out their new vision.

We were advocating something that was very new to the healthcare industry. We knew we needed to educate the market. When Marcus showed up and discussed his principles, it already fit into a paradigm that we believed. Doing the workshop with Marcus was the starting point of formally kicking off the process.

Phase 1: Uniting the Marketing and Sales Silos

Health Catalyst's first move was to implement the They Ask, You Answer methodology and draft up a list of the most common questions customers and clients ask. To get their list, the marketing team went to the sales team for answers.

Horstmeier noticed that the senior sales teams were being pulled in multiple directions, as they were traveling to meet clients and potential prospects to explain their services. He also noticed that the senior sales teams were already the experts in the field and could better manage their efforts as part of the content production initiative.

It was pretty easy for me to say, "We're going to create a marketing engine, and it's going to be all about education, and if you participate, it will relieve you of travel and reduce the demand on you. Because I'm going to create two ways, one via publishing and the other via webinars, to get your content out to thousands of people instead of tens of people."

It was so easy to catch the vision. We were fortunate in that the subject matter experts that we had on our team were subject matter experts nationally. We were in a new market and we were already the thought leaders, and we were already in demand.

For their first phase of content marketing, Horstmeier and his marketing crew leveraged the knowledge of their sales team to write compelling articles. However, after a few months of utilizing the sales experts and doing their own independent research, the marketing team surpassed the sales team as the thought leaders and relied less heavily on sales for content ideas.

Health Catalyst began to churn out three pieces of content each week, and in an industry nearly devoid of information, getting to the top of the first page on searches came pretty easily for the company.

> We have about 77 strategic keyword phrases that we target, and we own almost all of them. We have three segments of keywords. In our first segment, we have 95 percent of our words at the number 1 spot. In our two other segments we're at 50 percent. We have 100 percent of all the words on the first page of Google's search engine results with 50 percent of our words at the top position.

Another reason Health Catalyst's efforts have been so amazing is the way they have broken down the barrier between sales and marketing so that everyone is on board with the production and distribution of content. And it's not just *that* their sales team uses their content, but the *way* they do it.

Says Horstmeier:

> Our content team has grown. I have a core team, and I have a separate team that just writes "case studies." The sales team particularly uses the case studies. I've also created a tool on our website called "My Folder."
>
> This tool allows anyone (but the sales team uses it the most) to go onto our website, sort through whatever articles, case studies, or information they're looking for to give to a client and put those things in the "My Folder" tool. The salesperson can then send any file they add to the folder to a client.
>
> An automatic email is generated saying, "Hey, George, thank you very much for the meeting that we had. You asked for more info on XYZ. I've identified the three most important pieces of content I'd like you to read. Take a look and let me know what you think."

Phases 2 and 3: Live Webinars and Events

Producing regular content on their site was working very well for Health Catalyst, but they knew they could be doing more to educate the marketplace. Educating clients was extremely important to Health Catalyst. On the one hand, having all the information helped their sales team find new clients. On the other hand, Health Catalyst's product is pretty technical, and adequately explaining it so that clients purchased and used the product required making sure people were using it correctly.

For the second phase of Health Catalyst's marketing strategy, they began to implement regular live webinars for their clients, prospects, and anybody interested to attend their training sessions. All the webinars are free, and many have been recorded. Topics a potential client may be interested in are always available.

> What's pretty interesting about webinars is that everyone told us that in the healthcare industry the only way webinars would work is if we were featuring clients and not ourselves.
>
> But I knew that we had the thought leaders within our company. So we had a meeting and decided that our webinars would have a "content marketing mind-set," which would be all about educating and teaching. We didn't want to mention our company name much, if at all, because we try to teach principles and broaden the appeal of what we do.

Health Catalyst's education-over-promotion approach to webinars has paid off in a remarkable way, with an average sign-up for webinars between 600 and 700 people and as many as 1,200 people attending a single session.

In the third phase, Health Catalyst's created an industry event. One of the concerns that Horstmeier had about doing events was that, as a vendor and not a third party, hosting an event might come off as too promotional and not enough about educating the marketplace. Horstmeier agreed to host a health-care analytics summit under one very strict guideline—it must be an educational summit and not a Health Catalyst vendor event.

> The only mention during the whole summit of Health Catalyst was a small logo that said "powered by Health Catalyst." Unless you were really look-ing, you'd miss it.
>
> We were so committed to making it an analytics event and not a sponsored event that we asked everyone at the very end to vote on whether they thought it was a vendor event or an analytics event. Ninety-four percent of the people voted that we had kept our promise of making it about analytics and not Health Catalyst.

The transparency of their motives and their pledge to cultivate a cul-ture instead of building a brand has made them the trusted thought leaders in their space. When Health Catalyst hosted its first analytics summit, the expected attendance was between 100 to 250, and 620 people attended. Their second annual summit surpassed expectations once again.

> We just finished our second healthcare analytics summit. We widely expanded it. We had a capacity of 1,000 people, and we sold out six weeks ahead of time. We had to get approval to host any more people, so we ended up having 1,040 people there with 180 on the waiting list. And that was our second year.

Success and Plans for the Future

Health Catalyst's efforts have not only put them on the map, but also made them an industry thought leader. They built a marketing and sales strategy based on education, teaching, and transparency that transformed into a culture. And others in their field have taken notice:

> We've had several analysts give us an overall market review of our company, and they always put us at the top of the list. We had another analyst tell us that Health Catalyst's marketing was the most brilliant marketing campaign she'd ever seen in the industry.
>
> Our own president said, "In my 25 years in the healthcare field, I've never seen anything like this." Our clients are coming, and they're already educated. We walk into a meeting and they already know what we're doing. They've read our stuff. They've already asked questions. Many of them are ready to buy by the time we have our first meeting.

In just a little over two years, traffic to Health Catalyst's website has grown exponentially from a few thousand monthly visitors in August 2013 to more than 115,000 in October 2015, with most of the increase coming organically from solid search engine optimization (SEO) practices.

Today, the numbers are even higher, and they've clearly placed their stake in the ground as the foremost thought leader in the Healthcare Analytics space.

The Health Catalyst story is the ultimate example of a B2B industry where, instead of saying, "Hospitals don't find vendors on the internet," the organization embraced the idea that an obsession with education and transparency—in all its forms—could have a dramatic impact on the brand and business.

And boy, did it have an impact.

III

Implementation and Making It a Culture

Many companies have tried content marketing and failed.

Having spoken to so many companies on this subject, I've heard just about all the reasons why such failures occur. Not only that, but my consulting company has worked with dozens and dozens of businesses and brands to help them achieve greatness within their space.

Some have reach incredible heights of success.

Others have been a total bust.

As we've taken the time to separate the success stories from the busts, we've discovered there are four essential keys to making this work within any organization—ultimately, building the business, brand, and bottom line while becoming a true culture in the process.

In this part of the book, we break down these four keys, which are as follows:

- *Buy-in from top to bottom:* This is achieved through truly educating subject matter experts and key departments on the "what," "how," and "why" of content marketing.
- *Insourcing:* The process of utilizing company employees to produce content as part of their job descriptions.

- *The content manager:* Someone in the organization must own the effort and be fully dedicated to it (without distractions) to make it work.
- *Using the right tools:* Unless the right tools are used, it is extremely hard to calculate true return on investment (ROI) of the company's content marketing efforts.

33 | The Power of Insourcing and Using Your Team to Create Incredible Content

Truth be told, many, many organizations have tried embracing inbound and content marketing. One of the most common ways they do this is by engaging some type of digital marketing agency that produces their content for them. Although this concept of "outsourcing" your company's content production is by no means a bad thing, it can come with drawbacks.

A few reasons why follow.

For the most part, unless the content producer (for the agency) is embedded in the company, it is very difficult for that agency to reflect you, your brand, your brand story, and the subject matter expertise your company has accurately.

In many ways, your company's content and story represent the soul of your business. This being the case, it can be quite difficult for someone else to accurately reflect this "soul."

Also, agencies have a set "deliverable." For example, many may include something like "six blog articles a month" as part of their scope of work. On one hand, this is a very good thing because you know, as the client, that you're going to get six blog articles that month to publish to the site.

But on the other hand, the companies that have had the greatest success following the principles of They Ask, You Answer and content marketing generally aren't restricted by deliverables.

In other words:

- If they want to produce 10 blog articles in a month, they do it.
- If they want to create 12 videos in a month, they do it.
- If they want to write just one incredibly long and valuable blog post, they do it.
- If they want to revamp a portion of their website to better address buyer needs and concerns, they do it.

I hope you're seeing the point here. The creative flexibility to simply produce great content, in all its forms, without the limitations of a contract or deliverable, is a powerful, powerful thing.

Additionally, when a company is not dependent on an agency to "do the work," the team will learn it for themselves. Although the learning curve can mean slower results at first, the end results are often dramatically greater.

Finally, it's critical that your company's story and content be a true reflection of your sales messaging. This means, in a perfect world, that your sales team is very much involved in the selection and production of all of your company and brand content—more on this later.

Done right, when a prospect or customer contacts you, his or her first thought is: *"Yes, this is exactly who I thought they were. What they are saying is exactly what I read and saw."*

Ultimately, the question of producing your own content versus having someone else do it for you is much like the principle of the artist. Not until the artist is holding his or her own paintbrush can he truly produce a masterpiece. The same is true for any company wanting to become a thought leader in the digital age.

I stress again that there are many great agencies and outsourced writers out there who do produce great content. But the fact remains, if you want to be heard above the noise of your industry, you can't just be average. You can't be like everyone else in your space. ***You must do more, and you must do it better.***

Thus, owning your content effort, versus renting it out, can make all the difference.

The case studies and data my agency has on those clients who "owned" it versus those who "outsourced" it is empirical and incredibly clear—learning to do it in-house is the clearest path to exceptional results.

All of this leads to the opposite of outsourcing your company's content, something we call "insourcing," which we define as:

The process of using your existing employees and their knowledge about your services and products to produce educational content for the sales and marketing department—leading to better, buyer-centric content, more informed sales teams, and dramatically increased brand awareness.

34

Case Study 5

How Block Imaging Embraced a Culture of Insourcing

If you read the foreword of this book, you're familiar with the story of Block Imaging and Krista Kotrla. Krista wanted badly to turn Block Imaging around and knew that the principles of They Ask, You Answer would be the key not only to saving the business, but to making Block Imaging the leader of the medical imaging equipment space in the process.

But when she approached the sales and leadership departments of her organization, no one seemed to share her vision. The excuse? It was twofold:

"I don't have the time."
"That's not my job."

Let's look at both of these excuses for a second.

In life, when people tell you they "don't have time," what they're really trying to tell you, without actually telling you is: *"That thing you just explained to me is not as important to me as it is to you."*

In other words, they don't see its value.

The funny thing is, whenever we as humans or businesses see the value of something, we quickly start to make the time. In fact, "time" becomes a nonissue when profit and worth are identified.

155

The excuse of "That's not my job" is essentially the same. Today, if someone within an organization tells the marketing department, "It's not my job," he obviously doesn't understand what has happened with the shifts in sales and marketing in the digital age. The person doesn't understand the 70 percent number we discussed at the beginning of this book and just how much the buyer's journey has changed.

Again, people don't get it.

In Krista's case, neither management nor the sales department at Block Imaging understood the value of this incredibly important philosophy. Without question, the story of marketing departments not getting help from the rest of the team is prolific throughout the entire world today. And when I say "prolific," I am not exaggerating.

In fact, since I started writing and speaking about digital, the number one email I have received from readers—and it's number one by a long way—sounds something like this: *"Marcus, I am in marketing. I believe so much in using this honest, transparent teaching philosophy in doing business. But I just can't get management and sales to see what I see!"*

I have received hundreds of these types of emails over the years, and the sender's frustration is almost palpable.

The Silos Must Be Eliminated

Krista's dilemma is shared by most people in marketing—they understand their products, services, and buyers, they just don't understand them the same way sales or management does. Simply put, they are not (generally speaking) subject matter experts.

After all, the sales teams (among others in the organization) hear the main prospect and customer questions. It's also the sales team that is tasked with answering these questions. So if sales is on the front lines, why wouldn't they be included in the part of the sales process that has the greatest impact on the sale?

We keep telling marketing, *"Go and produce this content. Get us lots of leads. Move prospects down the funnel."* But to expect them to do so is ridiculous and outrageously improbable.

Understanding the *What,* the *Why,* and the *How*

When Krista asked me to come and speak to her company to help the various departments catch the vision that was inbound, content, and They Ask, You Answer, I knew it was a tremendous opportunity—for myself and for their team.

For the team because they would all be in a room, with their full focus and attention on understanding the what, how, and why of becoming the best teachers and educators in the medical imaging space.

For me because that was the first time I would go out and teach such a workshop—one focused on developing a true "culture" of They Ask, You Answer. Because I could see the workshop was going to have such an influence on Krista's team, and because I knew so many other "Kristas" who were out there struggling to achieve the same type of uniform vision and buy-in she was seeking, I knew my days of being a pool guy were numbered.

Since that day, I've taught hundreds of these same workshops around the globe, and the results have been extraordinary. The key to making them so effective comes down to three simple things:

- What is this thing we call content marketing?
- How does it work (They Ask, You Answer)?
- Why is it so important that everybody in the company participate?

Since that day with Block Imaging, Krista has had the help of well over 50 employees who have contributed to producing hundreds of articles, videos, and other content that have gone on the company website. But it all happened because they understood one key thing:

Everyone is a teacher, and everyone's voice matters.

When companies think this way, anything is possible. The marketing department changes. So does sales. Silos are eliminated. Culture and team-work are enhanced.

Just to help you really catch the vision of what is possible when things are done this way, read the following email Krista received from one of her sales team members in early 2016, five years after the original workshop:

Guys,

Y'all may be sick of hearing these stories, but I still get a kick out of it. I just had a conference call with a pain management center in Arkansas. Come to find out before we even spoke, the purchaser had printed off several of my blogs to bring to her board meeting. It enabled her to answer questions on comparison models, budgets, what equipment they needed, etc.

She had read and seen so much of our content, she said she couldn't wait to talk to me. She told me who my competitors were and how much they were quoting. Even when I told her we would likely charge more, she said, "But I trust you guys, I'd rather work with you."

I realize they don't all line up like this, but when our funnel is working at its best it is so so so sweet....I'm sure I could still find a way to screw up the deal, but the point is, I couldn't be better set up to succeed.

The effort to produce the content is WORTH IT! Thank you to the stellar efforts of the marketing team for really setting us apart.

Think about it, when was the last time your sales team sent an email to the marketing department that looked like this?

To close this chapter, here is a direct quote from Krista, speaking on the final results of They Ask, You Answer for Block Imaging:

*"Because of insourcing and content marketing, we can account for **at least $20 million in sales** we otherwise would never have gotten."*

35

Starting Off They Ask, You Answer with a Bang

Company Workshops

I hope that, by this point, you're excited about They Ask, You Answer.

You want your organization and brand to be seen as the most trusted thought leader of your space. You want to embrace insourcing and involve your team of subject matter experts. You want this philosophy to be a culture.

Of course, cultures aren't built on emails, announcements, and mission statements.

As you might imagine, if you finish this book, set it down, and then send out an email to your team that says, "Let's start answering customer questions and blogging," you will likely get nowhere quickly.

Again, your team must understand the *what, how,* and *why* of They Ask, You Answer, to allow what is a "program" in many people's eyes to eventually become a culture.

This is exactly why workshops (as well as long-term training) with the entire team are so critical to success. With every single business and brand I've worked with that has experienced exceptional results, a workshop has always been the key to kicking off the magic and creating a unified vision.

I discovered this first with Krista and her team at Block Imaging; I have since witnessed it more than 200 times in the workshops my team and I have taught to organizations, large and small, since 2011.

But if you want to give a workshop to help your team catch this vision, what is the best way to go about it? What are the key principles to focus on? What must the team clearly understand in order to start?

In this chapter, we answer these questions by showing you the eight essential principles participants must embrace from the very beginning in order to find the greatest success with content marketing and They Ask, You Answer—principles that are ideally taught in a workshop designed to lay out the entire vision of the content marketing efforts.

Principle 1: Buyer Expectations Have Changed

In this section of the workshop, the purpose is to shift the mind-set of each attendee into "buyer/consumer" mode. In other words, we want them thinking about the way *they* use the internet, how *their expectations* have changed when *they* are researching and vetting companies online, and the feelings *they* experience when a website doesn't give them what they're looking for.

Unless people have the ability to look in the mirror and analyze the way they shop, buy, and engage the web, it's very difficult for them to understand their prospects and customers at the level necessary.

Principle 2: The Way Search Engines Work

Here's a little secret: Outside of the tech/marketing world, *a large portion of people do not understand how search engines work.* Nor can they articulate how and why a search engine ranks and shows some sites (pieces of content) over others.

Ultimately, the key to this section of the workshop is to help every person realize that *the goal of search engines is to give its customer (the searcher) the best, most specific answer to a question (or need, problem, query, and so on) in that very moment.*

At the same time, even though Google wants to give great answers to their customers, most companies and industries don't embrace this "teacher" mentality online, leaving the reward to third-party websites that are more driven by consumer questions than by product pitches.

Principle 3: The Way Consumers Search and The Big 5

In the first part of the book, we discussed the critical nature of The Big 5 and how it drives consumer research around the world:

- Pricing and costs
- Problems
- Versus and comparisons
- Reviews
- Best in class

In this section of the workshop, the key is to help your team members reflect on all the times they've used each one of these phrases as keywords while they were shopping or researching online. If this is done correctly, people in the room will be nodding their heads again and again once they realize just how often they use The Big 5 in every aspect of their consumer-driven lives. By coming to this understanding, they'll also start to see how The Big 5 greatly apply to *their* existing prospects and customers.

If your organization is going to have great success with They Ask, You Answer, you cannot compromise in your desire to address all consumer questions. Regardless of how good, bad, or ugly the question may appear, if the marketplace is asking it, you must address it. And you must persuade your team to share this vision of wanting to address all queries versus retreating back to the old way of burying their heads in the sand, hoping the prospect never asks the question—ostrich marketing.

Principle 4: Group Brainstorming of Content Ideas

In this section of the workshop, the goal is to answer this question: *"What should we write about?"*

Instead of it being a science, the key is listening well, hearing the problems, questions, and needs of prospects and customers, and then addressing each one (be it via text, video, or other medium).

After attendees understand the They Ask, You Answer philosophy, as well as how it coordinates so perfectly with The Big 5, the next step is to have them apply what they've learned by brainstorming questions they receive every day from prospects and clients.

This activity can have a profound impact on all participants, and as you might imagine, it's usually dominated by those involved in sales, because they generally have the closest contact with existing and potential customers.

Principle 5: The Impact Content Can Have on the Sales Process and Closing Rates

Earlier, we said: "Employees need to understand 'why' they're being asked to participate in content marketing." Well, this section is a *huge* deal. As with everything else in life, people want to know WIIFT: ***What's in it for them.***

By seeing the dramatic impact great content can have on shortening the sales cycle while bringing in more qualified leads and greater margins, salespeople are generally *very* excited about the possibilities this principle can have on their bottom line and overall job performance.

Principle 6: The Reason Why Everyone's Voice, Talents, and Knowledge Are Critical for Success

The essence of the sixth is very simple: *Marketing should not be the digital voice of the company.* Marketing does not have its finger on the pulse of clients and customers like the rest of the company does. Therefore, marketing's job (from this point forward) is to help employees (who deal with customers or are subject matter experts) produce content (and therefore earn trust).

Essentially, each branch of the business needs to understand its overall value to the growth of the company and why it's critical that the marketing department is able to lean on them for teaching, information, and other pieces of content.

Principle 7: The Editorial Guidelines Going Forward

If employees are going to participate in the company's content marketing efforts, they'll need to understand what the entire process and corresponding expectations look like. Here are just a few questions and topics that should be covered:

- Who is the person in charge? (The title of this position varies, be it content manager, chief content officer, or other label.)
- How often will employees be asked to contribute content, and how often will they be required to meet with someone in marketing to produce said content?
- What are the different ways in which the employees will be able to contribute content—text, video, podcasts, etc.?
- What are the editorial guidelines for a typical blog post?

After employees are finished with this section of the workshop, they should have a clear roadmap in their heads of next steps, their individual roles, and expectations going forward.

Principle 8: A Look into the Future

This section of the workshop recaps everything that has been covered up to this point, including the benefits to the company as a whole and to each employee as well. Also, we have found that a very powerful discussion point in this section can be achieved by asking this simple question:

"What would prevent this culture of content marketing from working in our organization?"

I hope that this section has given you a better sense of what needs to be understood from day one to make the most out of They Ask, You Answer and establish a culture of content marketing. Keep in mind, too, that everything I've recommended is flexible and can be adjusted to meet the needs of your company or organization.

But the key, as always, is that *it happen*. Otherwise, resistance is likely on the horizon.

36

The Content Manager

Qualities to Look for, How to Hire One, and More

I hope that by this point in the book you're getting the message: "I need to do this." And if that's the impression you're getting, great, you're already on the way to becoming the most trusted voice and expert within your space.

But at the same time, to make it possible, it's more than just having the right strategy or getting the buy-in of your sales team.

Embracing content marketing and the philosophies of They Ask, You Answer is a big task, and unless someone owns it, it's very likely *not* going to work.

This "owner" can go by many names within an organization (especially based on how large the company is), such as:

- Chief content officer
- Content marketing manager
- Content manager
- Chief storyteller

- Brand journalist
- Inbound marketing manager
- And so on

Ultimately, though, the name doesn't matter.

The thing that does matter, though, is that he or she exists within the organization.

Often, when speaking to a marketer or CEO about turning content marketing and They Ask, You Answer into a culture, I'll have a conversation that sounds something like this:

MARKETING PERSON/CEO: I know we should be doing content marketing and following They Ask, You Answer. But I'm simply wearing too many other hats, and there is no way I can make the time for this myself.

ME: You need a content manager. Someone must *own* this effort and dedicate all his time to it, assuming you truly want to get exceptional results. (And for a larger organization, multiple content managers and editors should be dedicated to these efforts.)

MARKETING PERSON/CEO: I agree, but I think I can at least do some of this myself.

ME: Well, to be frank, you can't. At least, you won't do it very well. It will always play second fiddle to your other roles. I've seen it too many times.

MARKETING PERSON/CEO: But I'm just not sure the company is willing/able/ready/and so on to make this type of hire.

ME: And if you don't, again, it very likely won't work. Either you do this right or don't do it at all. You wearing another hat is only going to cause you more stress and produce few results...and that will lead to your team making false statements like, "We tried this content marketing stuff, but it didn't work for us."

I've had this very same conversation hundreds of times over the years, yet it keeps coming back again and again.

Someone Must Own It

Fact is, most businesses would rather dip their toes in the content marketing waters before they dive in. I get that. It's tempting. But just because something is tempting doesn't make it a good idea.

Here at IMPACT, as you've seen in the various case studies throughout this book, we've been blessed to watch many of our clients demonstrate exceptional success. But for all of these success stories, there is one commonality:

Producing great content is a full-time job, and someone has to own it.

Whenever we've allowed our clients to try this strategy without a true "owner" of the content, it hasn't worked out. Other priorities always took precedence. Production was too slow. The entire team never caught the vision.

But if we're being honest with ourselves, at this point in the game, knowing just how much the consumers and the buying process have changed, how could anyone deny the need to give the digital side of their business full attention?

Weekly Duties of a Content Manager

To better understand why this is a full-time position for at least one person (depending on the organization's size), let's look at what a typical week is like for an effective content manager.

With most of our clients, regardless of the size of their businesses, a "successful" week of content marketing will look like this:

- At least three new pieces of content (text, video, or audio): **5–15 hours**
- Company email marketing efforts: **1–3 hours**
- Site analytics, SEO, and so on: **3–5 hours**
- Social media engagement: **1–2 hours**
- Premium content production (ebooks, white papers, webinars): **3–5 hours**
- General website enhancements (new pages, call-to-action placement): **2–4 hours**
- Continual education/training (learning tools like HubSpot, new apps): **3–5 hours**
- Meeting with the sales team to discuss needed content, have training, and so on: **2–4 hours**

Depending on the organization, the industry, the customer base, and so on, all of these numbers can vary widely. This example is simply meant to give the reader a sense of the various responsibilities of a true content manager.

There are, of course, other duties, but I hope you can see just how quickly all these duties add up. For larger organizations, it's easy to fill these same tasks with multiple employees. For example, many of our clients not only have a content manager, but also a full-time videographer, full-time writers, and more.

And for each, the return on the investment of these positions has been more than worth it.

Choosing the Right Leader of Your Content Marketing Efforts

Let's assume you're ready to go all-in with content marketing and embrace the philosophy of They Ask, You Answer. Now that you're ready to hire a content manager, you must make sure that the hire is good. And when I say "good," I mean really, *really* good.

But what defines *good* in this case? What skill sets should you be looking for, especially when you're seeking to fill this position within your company? Here are what we have found to be the ten essential qualities of every successful content marketing manager (CMM); a list we use every time my team is tasked with hiring a CMM for an organization.

Ten Essential Qualities of Great Content Managers

1. **They love to write.** This one goes without saying, but it's a *big* deal. And remember, writing online isn't just about fancy words. It's about *clean communication*, done in a way that just about any reader can understand the content. Remember, great writers and communicators (and teachers) don't try to sound smart, which is never the goal of content marketing. Rather, they seek "communion," and this quality makes them great.

Furthermore, the individual must not only love writing, but also be fast, effective, and able to meet writing deadlines.

Without question, this skill is non-negotiable. Plus, remember this key:

You can always teach a great writer to be a good marketer, but you can't always teach a good marketer to be a great writer.

2. **They are skilled editors.** When companies leverage their existing employees to produce text and video content, the initial product can be "rough." But great content managers can take what is a 5 in terms of quality and make it a 9 or 10—making the original source as clear and concise as possible.

(Within a larger organization, this person would be considered an editor, but at the beginning, most content managers wear multiple hats, this being one of them.)

3. **They have excellent interviewing skills.** This is *huge*. Any legitimate organization is full of subject matter experts, but most of these same experts are not great writers and certainly not great content marketers.

Because insourcing is so critical to success, a great content marketing manager understands how to sit down with subject matter experts (and vendors as well) and ask the right questions to produce content that teaches, helps, and informs readers.

Furthermore, they can ask the questions from the consumer's or buyer's point of view—which is the absolute key to creating communion, understanding, and trust between buyers and businesses—the feeling of being "understood."

4. **They embrace social media and "get it."** It goes without saying that social media—in some form or another—is here to stay. Therefore, the mind-set of "I don't like social media" isn't the best one for a content marketing manager to have. In fact, it's a bad sign. Granted, social media, as discussed herein, isn't something every company should focus on, but they should be at least open and accepting of the possibilities.

5. **They have solid video editing skills.** Video just keeps getting bigger and bigger and bigger (more about this later in the book). In fact, for many of our clients at IMPACT, *video is way more important than text* when producing a heavy amount of content while attempting to utilize employees—especially those persons in the sales department.

In a perfect world, once a company is of any size, a full-time videographer will be hired to show the visual story of the company. But until that point, the content manager should have the ability to wear both hats, and with the ease of making, creating, and editing videos today, this is absolutely achievable.

6. **They are extremely likeable.** Do you remember the amazing success story of Krista Kotrla and Block Imaging? Among the many reasons Krista was so effective in exploding Block Imaging's brand and bottom

line, her likeability was a major factor. Her company's employees love her. She brightens their day, she has their respect, and because of this, they are quick to help with content marketing.

Frankly, when it comes down to it, unlikeable people make *awful* content marketing managers.

7. **They understand what makes people tick.** Again, when one is using employees as sources of content, knowing how to motivate and inspire said employees is critical. This is exactly why the best content managers know how to push the right buttons to give their employees the needed boost to contribute to the company's marketing and sales goals.

8. **They are organized and goal oriented.** Content marketing needs to have *order*. This starts with a main editorial calendar and continues with newsletters, trainings, interviews, and so on. All of these elements require order, planning, and organization.

9. **They love analytics, numbers, and measurement.** As I've worked closely with so many CEOs and marketers on their content marketing over the past few years, I keep seeing a simple trend: Those persons who pay attention to the numbers get *wayyyyy* more results.

This is another reason why a content marketing manager needs to become skilled not just with Google Analytics, but also with other tools, such as HubSpot, and others.

(You can see a list of the best content tools we recommend at impactbnd.com/tools.)

10. **They are continually thinking outside the box.** Look around at some of the greatest content marketing examples and I'll show you creativity and unique thinking every time. Fact is, the best ones in this industry aren't looking for a set of rules or a road map that tells them exactly what they need to do next.

Instead, *they just get stuff done,* however they possibly can, often with some serious creativity acting as the catalyst to success.

Trained Journalists May Be a Perfect Match for Your Content Marketing Needs

As you look at those 10 qualities, it's pretty obvious why the journalism industry has taken content marketing by storm. In fact, at my agency, almost all of the hires for content marketing managers for our clients come directly from this industry; the majority are recent journalism graduates, ready for work, and perfectly suited to meet this position's demands at a very reasonable price. Granted, they do need to receive the necessary training to "think like a marketer" and embrace the philosophy of They Ask, You Answer, but there is no question, assuming they are good, about whether they can get the job done.

With so much of this talent available (because of the dying newspaper industry), there is really no excuse for companies not to fill their content marketing positions and start receiving the benefits to their business, brand, and bottom line immediately.

Also, keep in mind that as I write this, I realize not every company can afford to hire a full-time content manager. I was a perfect example of that with River Pools and Spas, when I embraced They Ask, You Answer in 2009. But it was for that very reason I worked at my kitchen table producing content almost every single night from 10 p.m. to 1 a.m. for two straight years.

In my case, I didn't have a choice. But knowing what I know now and seeing what I've seen, I say that if you do have a choice, get the right people in the right seats from the beginning.

You may be asking what specific tests you can use to choose the right content manager during the hiring process. Because we've done so much of this at IMPACT, we have found certain activities to be very effective, and we also have found a few things you should be paying close attention to.

How to Make Sure Your Potential Content Manager Is the Right Fit for Your Company and Brand

I *really* emphasize finding someone who totally embodies your top five organizational values. The person is going to be writing on behalf of the brand "voice," so you want the writing to reflect an effortless, one-and-the-same brand personality.

You might have potential candidates perform the following exercises during the vetting and hiring process:

- Ask them to turn a really poorly written rough draft into a nice article.
- Give them only an outline of an article and ask them to turn it into two full-blown articles.

- Give them a list of blog titles and have them write the interview questions they would use to interview an expert to complete the article.
- Give them a "question" that acts as the main subject of a video or blog post. Now, instead of you interviewing them, have them interview you (either in front of the camera or simply by taking notes), to get a full and thorough answer for the question. Once the interview is finished, give the candidate a short window (24 to 48 hours) to return with a completed blog post (or video) answering the question.

As you might imagine, this final activity is extremely effective in the selection process because it tests the candidate on multiple fronts: their abilities to interview well, think on their feet, ask great questions, meet deadlines, and produce solid content.

I also suggest having several people from your team interview the candidate just to make sure he or she is likable and gets along well with everyone.

And finally, make note of their personal interests. Do they write for fun? Are they into producing their own videos? Do they consistently use social media as well? Do they have creative hobbies? Do you sense they are called to create and grow something of their own?

Remember, the tools and the strategy can be taught. The values, curiosity, and natural passion for both people and writing are critical to making all of this come together and ultimately to achieve greatness.

37

The Importance of Having the Right Tools

Measuring Return on Investment, the Power of HubSpot, and More

As we've established, They Ask, You Answer is a business philosophy that guides the sales and marketing approach of an organization through obsessive listening, teaching, and a desire to solve the problems of the marketplace.

For this philosophy to work, a few things have to happen:

- There must be shared buy-in.
- Departments must be aligned.
- Everyone has to understand the underlying vision.
- Great, quality-driven content needs to be produced through text, audio, video, and other media.

But after all of this is done, it's critical that a business can answer the following question: ***But did it make us any money?***

If your organization is going to spend the time, resources, and money needed to make content marketing and They Ask, You Answer work, there absolutely should be an ongoing understanding of the company's return on investment (ROI).

And in case you hadn't noticed, the principle of showing ROI has been a major part of this book and the case studies herein.

Whether it was the "How Much Does a Fiberglass Pool Cost?" article that generated more $6 million in revenue for River Pools, or Krista's statement of "$20 million in additional revenue" with Block Imaging—the numbers have been a major part of the discussion, as well they should be.

You see, the fact is, as businesses, *we must make money.*

And then we must turn a profit.

All this They Ask, You Answer stuff is nice, but without it helping you to seriously generate more revenue for your company, it's not worth the price tag on the cover. It is for this reason that, with digital sales and marketing, tools do matter—a lot.

When I was a struggling pool guy on the brink of losing my business in early 2009, I spent quite a bit of time reading about digital marketing and how such things as content marketing, blogging, and so on could make such a big difference on a business's bottom line.

Although I found many helpful websites during this time period, the one place I kept going back to again and again was a startup "marketing automation" software called HubSpot.

Since the early days when I was learning from the company, HubSpot has become somewhat famous in the world of marketing for a phrase their two founders—Brian Halligan and Dharmesh Shah—championed from the beginning of the company: "inbound marketing."

As they explained it to me in 2009, "inbound" marketing was essentially the opposite of old-school "outbound" marketing. It was about providing value (through information) to consumers online, leading them to come to you (inbound) versus the traditional method of bombarding consumers with interruption-based content like TV, radio, print advertising, and so on.

For me, the message was obvious and something we needed to do, which is exactly why we embraced our They Ask, You Answer philosophy.

Because they had done so much to educate me on the way inbound marketing worked, HubSpot had gained my trust. And because of this, using their software to measure our success and enhance our inbound efforts only made sense.

So despite the fact that we didn't have the money to pay for it, we signed up for HubSpot in March 2009.

Since that time, the impact that tools like HubSpot have had on River Pools and Spas, as well as our clients at IMPACT, has been phenomenal. Specifically, in this chapter we discuss the three major benefits we've encountered, benefits that every business must consider if they truly want to reach their online potential:

- The ability to measure ROI
- The ability to track lead behavior
- The ability to test your website

1. The Continuous Ability to Measure ROI of Your Digital Marketing Efforts

This is a big, big deal. As mentioned, if you're going to embrace content marketing and They Ask, You Answer—and spend the time, effort, money, and so on, to make it work—you need to see returns.

And when I say "returns," I'm not just talking about visitors or leads to your website. *We're talking sales and revenue.*

By using a tool like HubSpot, whenever anyone on your website fills out a form (contact form, ebook download form, and so on), you have the ability to "track" that person—specifically, his or her IP address. With this tracking, you're able to see the major data points that will allow you to measure ROI—the first page of the site a person landed on and how he got there in the first place.

The reason why first-page-landed-on is so important is that if someone is using a search engine like Google and lands on that page and then eventually goes so far as to become a customer—you can trace the customer's first visit to the website back to that page, therefore giving that page credit for the sale and revenue numbers.

It is for this reason I was able to say that the article, "How Much Does a Fiberglass Pool Cost?" generated our company more than $6 million in revenue. It is also for this reason that every case study you've read up to this point in the book has done the same—showing true revenue numbers for ROI.

Aside from first-page-viewed, it's also critical when measuring ROI to know what website (or means) brought the visitor to your website.

For example, many companies today use pay-per-click (PPC) advertising (like Google Ads) to generate traffic to their websites. Whenever I'm discussing this subject with a company and they tell me they're using PPC, my first question is: *"How much money did it make your company last year?"*

Sadly, many companies can't answer this critical question, because they're not using the right tools.

At River Pools, despite the fact that we're able to generate a couple million organic website visitors a year to our website, we still engage in pay per click advertising, and here are the results:

In 2015, we spent $12,000 on pay per click, which equated to 11,657 website visitors, 437 leads, 33 sales appointments, and seven customers. These seven customers generated $357,000 in total revenue, with a net profit of just under $100,000.

In other words, for us, PPC is worth it. But had we not been using a tool like HubSpot, this type of data would not be available to us, leading to guesswork and a possible misallocation of marketing funds.

While working with our various clients at IMPACT, we've seen time and time again that some companies who thought PPC was worth it were actually losing money, while others who thought PPC didn't make financial sense were missing out on major revenue opportunities.

But PPC is just one example of many. The same story could be told for social media. In the world of digital sales and marketing, companies are continually debating the efficacy of social media, yet few are able to say: *"Because of Facebook, we generated a net profit of $X million for our company last year."*

No company, regardless of how big or small, can "do everything well" with content, social media, PPC, etc. It is for this reason that organizations need to study and measure what truly drives revenue, and use that data to help them focus more energy and efforts on what's generating the most revenue for the organization while spending less energy and effort on that which has the smallest returns.

2. The Ability to Track Lead Behavior and Use This Advanced Intelligence Throughout the Sales Process

Along with measuring ROI, the other major benefit of using a tool like HubSpot has to do with advanced lead intelligence. And when I say "advanced lead intelligence," I'm referring to having the ability to know what pages of the website a lead has seen, how many times the lead visited the site, and how long she spent on each page.

For many sales professionals, the first time they call or contact a lead is a "blind" conversation. They don't yet know much about the lead, her needs, her hot buttons, and so on. But with advanced lead intelligence, a sales pro can now see every page of the website that individual has read, every video she's watched, and know every time she's come to the site. Digging deeper, each one of these pages is a reflection of what the lead is or is not interested in.

For example, in my case with River Pools, if I saw a lead had visited the "How to Finance a Swimming Pool" page once, I knew he was likely going to need to find financing for a pool. If he looked at the page twice, it was an absolute guarantee he was going to need financing.

By knowing this, I could work to ensure the lead had financing taken care of *before* I drove up to his or her home for the sales appointment, a simple act that would dramatically increase closing rates.

The key to remember here is that every lead has his or her own story—a story that writes itself as the lead engages your content, thus showing you what truly matters and what does not.

For any seasoned sales professional, this type of knowledge and intelligence is very, very appealing.

3. The Ability to Test Your Website

The last major benefit of using of using an advanced analytics tool like HubSpot is your ability to test what is and what is not working on your website to convert more leads. For example, most websites have various "calls-to-action" statements or buttons (like "click here" or "download now") sprinkled throughout the site.

Notwithstanding, most companies never test these calls-to-action to see how such things as the color of the button, or the wording used, affects conversion rates—how often someone fills out a form.

With our clients at IMPACT, we've seen time and time again situations when we thought a page's copy, design, or call-to-action were just right, only to make some minor changes and see a major lift in lead conversions in the process.

Too often, we look at a website and because we think "it looks right," we think that it's performing at its highest level.

The reality is the best companies understand that *just because something **looks** right doesn't mean it **is** right,* nor does it mean changes aren't needed.

By having a culture of testing within the digital side of your business, you'll see again and again that the simplest changes in words, messaging, colors, and design matter—and therefore deserve your attention as a business.

This chapter could easily have been much longer, especially with the rate of change in tools and technology today. It's also important to note that HubSpot is only one of many types of software that give you the ability to do the things we discussed here.

That being said, the core theme is that *we should all be measuring*, so that at any point in your efforts to become the thought leader of your space and embrace They Ask, You Answer you're able to say:

"We put in a lot of work, but we know how much money it made. And it was well worth it."

PART

IV

Creating a Culture of Video… In-House

A few years ago, just before *They Ask, You Answer* was released the first time, I was bothered by a trend I was seeing in the marketplace:

Video was becoming a fundamental part of the buying process, and almost no businesses seemed to know how to deal with the shift.

It's not that these businesses didn't see the power of video, but rather the idea of video production—at least in-house—seemed completely unattainable to them.

And, time and time again, I saw a pattern of businesses making the same mistake. They would spend thousands and thousands of dollars to hire a video production company, only to walk away with a couple of videos, a gaping hole in their marketing budget, and not much else to show for it.

Knowing the financial miracle we were able to pull off at River Pools was a direct result of having learned and done all of these digital marketing activities in-house, I went to my team at IMPACT and posed a simple question:

"Can we teach companies how to create a culture of video in-house, without them needing to outsource anything?"

The reactions to my question were mixed:

"Marcus, that's never been done before."

"If we're not producing it for them, how could it be a viable business model for us as an agency?"

"Most companies will fail if they do this themselves."

I pushed back:

"Why not? Why couldn't we be the first firm to truly 'teach' organizations how to embrace a culture of video in-house? This is obviously where the world is headed, and so what if no one else is doing it? It's what's needed. And it's the right thing to do."

With that, an incredible journey began. We threw ourselves into video and decided to teach it just as we had taught inbound and content marketing—start with sales in mind, and the rest will fall into place.

And fall into place it did.

Today, hundreds of clients around the globe have embraced the mindset of "We are all media companies."

It turns out that I wasn't alone in thinking that this needed to be done, and there *was* a market for it. A lot of business owners and CEOs felt exactly as I did—that ownership of video would be critical to their success in the years that lie ahead.

Even better, video is the ultimate expression of They Ask, You Answer. Buyers want it. And not only do they want it (as we'll discuss later), but more and more prefer to learn visually over simply reading a textual explanation.

In the following pages, we're going to answer two major questions about video:

*What types of videos actually get results from a **sales** perspective?*

What must a company do to create a culture of in-house video?

We won't be able to answer all of your questions here. We will, however, give you a clear sense as to what actions and steps you can take right now within your business to see quick and powerful results from video.

At the end of this section, we'll reference links that will allow you to take a deeper dive into some of the more important subjects and questions surrounding video.

Finally, keep your eyes open for a new book coming soon—*The Visual Sale*. *The Visual Sale* will present a comprehensive deep-dive into how companies around the world are using video to revolutionize their approach to sales and marketing to grow their businesses.

What follows, however, will lay the foundation for your journey with video.

38

We're All Media Companies and the Visual Sale

The stats on video are profound. Even since the first edition of *They Ask You Answer*, the developments in video have been astounding. Although we could analyze video stats and trends for the next few pages to convince you that "video really is a big deal," I'd rather we cut to the chase and address the "what" and "how" of video—going beyond the "why."

However, for those stat lovers out there who thirst for empirical data and "proof," let's chew on this one: ***A recent study by Cisco found that, globally, video traffic will be 82 percent of all consumer internet traffic by 2022, up from 75 percent in 2017.***

In other words, of all the time we spend on the internet consuming content, the vast majority of that content is video.

It's easy to hear numbers like that and immediately dismiss them as flash-in-the-pan trends that will quickly fizzle out. In fact, I'm still astounded by the number of people who tell me, "I don't watch video online, and if I don't watch it online, why would my customers?"

If there is one thing I've learned over the past 10 years of embracing digital and the principles of They Ask, You Answer, and am definitively clear on, it is this: ***We should never let our personal opinions screw up smart business choices.***

At this point, video has nothing to do with whether or not we like it, use it, or can imagine our customers using it. The marketplace has spoken. Video is not slowing down any time soon.

But let's go back to this 82 percent statistic for a second. What percentage of your website, right now, is video-based? If you're like most organizations I speak with, you're likely in the range of 0 to 10 percent. This may make you feel as if there is no hope, but take comfort in the fact that, if you're at 0 to 10 percent, your competitors are right there with you as well.

There is no better time than right now to embrace video and visual selling, and all the benefits that will come from those efforts. But you cannot be passive.

Let me repeat that.

When it comes to video, you must not be passive; it's not an option.

Don't misunderstand me. I'm not saying you need to go out and buy a video production company to be successful. Instead, you must be the catalyst for a shift within your organization about how you view your future and the impact video will have on it.

To that end, the mindset that we teach all of our readers and clients at IMPACT—which continues to generate the greatest results—is this: *We are all media companies, whether we like it or not.*

For example, River Pools is a media company that happens to sell swimming pools. IMPACT is a media company that happens to offer digital sales and marketing services. The same is true for your business.

I know, such a mindset sounds like a contradiction but, given the needs and wants of today's digital buyers, it is the inescapable evolution we must all make. The moment we acknowledge we're a "media company," we start making decisions much differently.

Just as They Ask, You Answer forces you as a business to think like a buyer, seeing yourself as a media company starts with an essential philosophy: *Unless we show it, it doesn't exist.*

Think about that for a second. How much of your business is stated but not shown? Media companies recognize that the more they show, the more buyers will appreciate their transparency and willingness to teach—and that ever-important trust we seek to earn from consumers will inevitably follow.

This mindset and philosophy should permeate every aspect of your business—especially sales, marketing, and the customer experience. To help you, we'll break down the fundamental elements of becoming a media company and show exactly how you can create a culture of video in-house.

Yes, you read that correctly—*in-house*.

After all, you are a media company, aren't you?

39

The Selling 7

7 Videos That Will Immediately Impact Sales and Closing Rates

As we've already said, inducing *trust* is the main reason for a business to use any form of selling video. But once you move past trust and pose the question of "why," the answer should always start with sales, *not* marketing.

*That's right. Video is a **sales** initiative.*

Whether you're B2B, B2C, service, product, e-commerce, or whatever, your goal is to induce enough trust to make more sales for your organization. This is why your sales team should feel as if almost every video you create is another tool in their toolbox that will lead them closer to their goals. Fact is, they should be *thrilled* when they hear another video has been produced.

Sadly, too often when companies produce video content, they don't focus on what actually generates the greatest ROI and trust. As a result, the sales team often believes those videos are "marketing fluff," presenting little to no use in the sales process.

For example, the number one video we see companies invest in and create first is the "about us" video. "About us" videos may be nice, but when was the last time your sales team said: *"I can't wait to start using our new 'about us' video in my sales pitch!"*

Likely never.

What sales is looking for, as you know, is content that will overcome prospect concerns, address common fears, and clearly answer buyer questions. If we were looking at this in terms of the traditional buyer's funnel, we would focus on the types of videos that are aligned with the bottom of the funnel. What do *buyers* really want to know?

Furthermore, if your organization is going to invest time, effort, and resources into video production, then eventually your CFO, controller, or accountant is going to ask a critical question: *"Is this video stuff actually making us any money?"*

If the answer is "no" or "I'm not sure," then you have a serious problem. "About us" videos are the ultimate "I'm not sure." Even the best intentions in business will eventually be cut off or eliminated if their value is not proven.

This is why, ideally, your sales team should be saying, *"I couldn't come close to being as effective as I am if we weren't producing this video content."*

Additionally, your prospects should be raving to you about how helpful your videos were during the research process. If this isn't happening, again, you have a problem.

But now let's move to action, shall we? Let's say we agree that videos should be created to help the sales team **right now**, and we're ready to get started. What comes next?

That's where The Selling 7 comes into play. The Selling 7 was created over the course of a few years (and a few hundred B2C and B2B client case studies) with our team at IMPACT. Because we were in uncharted waters teaching how to use in-house video, we knew most clients would need to see quick results.

Otherwise, and understandably so, they would pull the plug. *Thus, The Selling 7 was born.* Once you read about each of these, your initial reaction will very likely be, "OK, this is a no-brainer. Why aren't we already doing this?"

But as is often the case in business, we overcomplicate very simple truths.

40

The Selling 7, Video 1

The 80 Percent Video

If you ask sales teams what percentage of the questions they hear on a sales call are exactly the same from call to call, the vast majority will give you a number between 70 and 90 percent. That's because sales teams answer the same questions over and over again, day in and day out. And it can get pretty old.

Ask any sales professional, *"What are the questions you are commonly asked that tell you a prospect is clearly **not** ready to buy?"*

They will recite an extensive catalog of those questions. Anyone who has been in sales for any period of time understands this all too well.

But what would happen if, every time you had a sales call, not only did your prospect already know the answer to those too-common questions, but had seen it, heard it, and learned it from *you*? Yep, the sales appointment would be *dramatically* more productive. And not just more productive, but much shorter, too.

Now, instead of spending so much time answering universal questions, you could address your prospect's specific questions that are unique to their needs and circumstances. You also wouldn't have to spend nearly as much time building relationships of trust on the front end of the appointment because it will have been established long before you shake the prospect's hand.

This is exactly why the 80 percent video is so imperative for sales success.

Putting It into Action

The 80 percent video process is simple:

- Brainstorm a list of the most important products and/or services your company offers. Eventually, you will create an 80 percent video for each.
- Have your sales team (or anyone who deals with a prospect) brainstorm the most common questions they hear on a typical sales call regarding that particular product or service. At a minimum, you should be able to come up with 10 questions.
- Once you've completed your brainstorming, narrow your list down to the top seven questions. These will constitute your core "80 percent." (If you're wondering whether or not you can choose more or less than seven, the answer is yes. We've simply found with our own clients that seven tends to be the most effective number.)
- Answer each question in an individual video. This video can—and generally should—be uploaded to your company's YouTube page and utilized anywhere else that is potentially helpful to buyers on your website.
- Take these seven videos and combine them into one long video. This will be your 80 percent video.
- Immediately get this video into the hands of your sales team and integrate it into the sales process, with the core purpose being to have prospects view it *before* the initial appointment.

As you might imagine, the 80 percent video is incredibly effective when done properly.

Chances are, however, if you're like most clients or audiences we speak to, you have some questions at this point. Because this video is so monumentally important to your business going forward, we're going to take some time here to thoroughly cover the questions you're going to run into once you start producing this type of video.

Do not skim this section.

Your understanding of seemingly "inconsequential" details will be the difference between achieving massive success and experiencing pitiful results.

Common Questions Regarding the 80 Percent Video

1. **How long should the 80 percent video be? Aren't you afraid the prospect won't watch something long?** One of the most ridiculous notions in the history of the internet is the idea that "all videos should be short" or that "all videos should be less than 90 seconds." Yes, it is true that when a video extends beyond 90 seconds, the watch rates dip. But the same is true after the first three seconds of watching a video. But does that mean all videos should be three seconds? Of course not.

Our philosophy at IMPACT, one that has worked incredibly well for hundreds of clients, is simple: *Answer the question as concisely, yet thoroughly, as possible.*

Yes, you read that correctly. We want them to be *concise* in the way they communicate—to the point, clear, and incisive. But we also want them to be *thorough* enough to empower the prospect or buyer to say by the end, "Perfect. Now I understand."

By adhering to this philosophy, you won't have to spend so much time debating the frustrating question "How long should this video be?" Instead you can start getting to work. When it comes to optimal length of video, far and away the most significant factor is where the buyer is in the sales cycle.

For example, if you just started thinking about buying a swimming pool last night, you likely only want to watch short videos or read shorter content on the subject. But, if you know that a salesperson is coming to your house tomorrow, and that you might sign a contract for $50,000 to $100,000 for a swimming pool, there is a very, very good chance you'd be more interested in watching a longer video. In fact, our average customer at River Pools has watched more than 20 minutes of River Pools–produced video before they buy.

We've seen this trend with buyer watch-time replicated in many other industries as well, and it's not just about price. What's more, price isn't even the variable that best dictates how much video someone is willing to watch. Rather, it comes down to this: *How great is their fear of making the wrong decision?*

When we're afraid to make a wrong decision, we will spend as much time as it takes to get comfortable with our buying choices. This is the reality of the digital age.

2. **Should one person or multiple people act as subject matter experts in an 80 percent video?** The primary goal for any video you produce is that the communication be clear, effective, and helpful. If this means that you need to choose the one person on staff that is capable of this, then by all means, use that one person. That being said, in a perfect world, it often comes across as very impressive to the viewer when multiple subject matter experts from your company play a part in these videos. Again, it's not a must, but it does make a difference.

You'll also find that some salespeople want to create their own 80 percent videos for prospects. This certainly makes sense—at least in terms of their relationships with the prospect—and as long as the quality meets your company's brand standards, then it's likely a good thing. It also sets an example to the rest of the sales team that one of their peers is going above and beyond to build trust as quickly and as strongly as possible in the relationship.

3. **What if we offer hundreds (if not thousands) of products or services? Do we have to create a video for each?** Obviously, it's unlikely that you're going to be able to create hundreds of 80 percent videos if your company sells hundreds of products. Of course, if you do have multiple products and services that you offer, ask yourself:

- What are the 20 percent of products and/or services that we sell that generate 80 percent of the revenue? (Pareto's Law)
- What are the products and/or services that have the greatest untapped potential and opportunity for our organization?

Just by answering these two questions, you'll have a strong sense of which products and services need to come first.

4. **What should a salesperson say to ensure that more prospects actually watch the video before a sales appointment?** We talked about this in our chapter on assignment selling, but it's too important not to mention again. Since the book was originally published, we've seen that most sales teams still struggle with properly using content (text, video, podcasts, and so on) in the sales process.

Case in point, most salespeople invite prospects to watch video using incredibly weak language, as demonstrated in the following: *"We have some excellent videos on our website. It would be great if you could watch a few of them before our next meeting."* That's not effective. It's a passive suggestion.

Here is an ideal script that your sales team can follow:

SALESPERSON: Mr. Jones, I know it's important to you that when we meet to discuss [product/service] that we don't waste any of your time. Not only that, I'm sure it's safe to say you don't want to make any mistakes along the way. To ensure you don't make any of the common mistakes we see buyers make, we've created a video that addresses the top seven questions and concerns people just like you have when making this type of decision.

By watching this video, you'll save time and money and eliminate the stress of potential buying mistakes. Plus, our time together will be dramatically more productive and effective. Will you take the time to watch this video before our meeting on Friday?

In the above sample script, the salesperson clearly states the value of the video in terms that lead with the needs and desires of the buyer. Moreover, the call-to-action is direct and time-bound.

5. **Can this video be used in customer service?** Not only can you use 80 percent videos within your customer service department, but you absolutely *should* use them. Using video to quickly show customers how to fix or solve their customer service issues can save many thousands of dollars per year in unnecessary expenses. To do this, find the most common (80 percent) customer service issues you're having with the major products and services that you offer. Then use these videos as part of your "purchase package" when on-boarding new customers.

6. **How does this type of video apply to e-commerce, when there is no "salesperson" involved?** Sadly, many companies believe that because they're e-commerce, the 80 percent videos concept doesn't apply to them. This couldn't be further from the truth. In a perfect world, every major product you sell in e-commerce has an 80 percent video that is shown right there with it, readily available to shoppers to watch and resolve their most pressing questions and concerns.

7. **Should these videos just be "talking head" style, or does there have to be more production value?** Always remember, "some" is better than "none" when it comes to educational videos. In other words, a basic talking head video is much more effective than a robust, production-driven video that has never been published because it's lost in production purgatory.

That being said, over time, you will want to make improvements to your 80 percent video, especially when using b-roll (shots of the product or service, or even your people), to make it more visually clear, whatever you're trying to explain to the viewer. But don't be afraid to start basic and allow organic progress and growth from there.

8. **What are the most common mistakes companies make with the 80 percent video?** As you may have gathered from other areas of this book, the biggest mistake companies make with their 80 percent video is that they overcomplicate the process. Typically, this occurs when they're too busy thinking like a business and not nearly busy enough thinking like an actual buyer. (The same rule holds true for the rest of the video types.)

Great communication in any video, but especially in the 80 percent video, has a tone that sounds something like:

"If you're considering _____, we know you have questions. You may even have concerns. But you can stop worrying because that's why we created this video. We want you to be informed. We also want you to be relaxed. So let's address your concerns—and by the end of this video, you'll likely have a much better understanding of the answers to the questions that have been on your mind."

The other major mistake companies make is that they don't state questions as the buyer would but as they, the business, would. Let's look at a quick example if you were selling a swimming pool.

Bad: "Why getting a diving board is a bad idea."
Good: "Is getting a diving board right for me and my family?"

Notice, the first one is biased, with a clearly stated opinion. The second is open and unbiased, written exactly as a potential buyer would articulate the question, if he or she were debating on a diving board for a swimming pool.

9. **Can the 80 percent video be used throughout the sales process, not just before the first appointment?** *Yes!* One of the greatest benefits of this video type is its ability to influence other decision-makers who aren't present for actual sales conversations. So often, sales are lost because the "messenger"—the individual who actually spoke with the salesperson—is unable to explain to the rest of the decision-makers

the value of the product or service or address their core questions regarding the product.

You see this a lot in the sales world. For example, let's say one spouse was physically present for a sales appointment but the other wasn't able to attend. When this occurs, often the spouse who was in attendance is left explaining (and therefore selling) to the other spouse the product's features, benefits, value proposition, and so on.

As you can well imagine, this is a salesperson's worst nightmare, and is one of the biggest reasons why an apparent "hot lead" can go cold so quickly. Leveraged properly, the 80 percent video can and should fill this void.

41

The Selling 7, Video 2

Bio Videos for Email Signatures

At its core, video, done correctly, can humanize your business in a powerful way. In a perfect world—in which you are using video well—potential customers and buyers are able to see, hear, and know you and your employees before the first handshake.

One of the best and simplest ways to humanize your business is by creating what we refer to as a "bio" video for each of your team members—especially those who are customer facing.

A bio video accomplishes two goals:

- It explains what the person does for the company or what he or she loves about his or her job.
- It also gives a little bit of personal information about what the person does when not at work.

By mixing a bit of personal and professional in a short video—typically 90 to 120 seconds long—you now have the ability to introduce yourself much earlier in the sales process.

Although a bio video can be used in a variety of ways, such as on your "team" or "about us" pages of your website, we have found that the most effective place for this video is in your email signature. Email signatures are dramatically underused and under-appreciated areas of digital real estate as a sales and marketing tool. But their benefits can be significant.

If you were to look at a typical email signature, most people have the basics—name, company, contact information, social media profiles, and possibly an image of a face.

By also placing a bio video in this signature—with a clear thumbnail image denoting it's a video—you give your email recipients a chance to get to know you on a visual, and therefore human, level.

As we've helped implement these simple videos with sales teams around the world, we've consistently found an average of 25 to 30 additional views per month of the video when it's integrated into an email signature. Think about that for a second—that's 25 to 30 more people who now know your name, your face, your voice, and your story.

We've all heard a million times that we "buy from those we know, like, and trust." Bio videos, when used properly, can help you drastically increase your odds of closing a deal by fostering closer connections between you and your prospects.

Common Questions Regarding Bio Videos

1. **Who should be required within a company to have a bio video? What types of employees or positions?** Usually, we suggest to clients that they require each of their sales team members to have a bio video. Because relationship-building is such a critical part of sales, this only makes sense. Anyone else who is customer-facing or is a member of your leadership team should strongly consider utilizing a bio video as well.

2. **Where else can bio videos reside?** Other than email signatures, the best place for this type of video is on the "about us" or "team" pages of your website. In fact, in certain industries—for instance, medicine or healthcare—the "meet the team" page is often one of the most viewed pages of the website. Beyond this, employees can and should integrate this video into their social media channels, especially LinkedIn.

3. **Can employees produce these themselves on their phones, or does there need to be more of a production element involved?** As always, we advocate that attempting to do (and learn) video is a good thing for any organization and its employees. That being said, if you have a choice to make the videos look and feel more professional, then of course you should do that.

42

The Selling 7, Video 3

Product and Service Fit Videos

When it comes to the traffic on most organizations' websites, one of the most viewed sections is commonly what are considered "product" or "service" pages. The way these pages are designed, at least from a messaging standpoint, is often extremely flawed. Why? Because all these pages tend to do is espouse why the product or service is great, what it is, what it does, etc.

But for those businesses that understand the way buyers actually think (embracing a They Ask, You Answer mindset), there is an essential second type of information this page must include, simply: *Who is the product or service **not** for?*

Yes, you read that correctly—*not* for.

Now, you may be wondering why. Think about it—the minute we are willing (as businesses) to say what we're not is the precise moment we become dramatically more attractive to those for whom we are a good fit. Therein lies the key to a product or service fit video. It explains who the product is—and is not—a good fit for in the most honest and transparent way possible.

If you follow the They Ask, You Answer model of The Big 5 and The Selling 7, the product and service pages of your website will list some (if not all) of the major questions buyers ask during the buying process and have a video that clearly answers the question, "But is it right for me?"

Common Questions Regarding Product and Service Fit Videos

1. **Can it be used in applications other than product or service pages?** *Yes!* That's the beauty behind The Selling 7. Just as the name suggests, their most effective use cases are often found by sales teams as they leverage them throughout different stages of the sales process.

2. **How long should a fit video be?** Unlike the 80 percent video, which addresses multiple questions, a product or service fit video is really only addressing two—who or what is a good fit, and who or what is a bad fit? Therefore, in most cases, this video will be shorter than five minutes. As is always the case, this number will vary drastically depending on the complexity of the answer.

3. **What are the biggest mistakes companies make with a fit video?** The biggest issue we've seen with clients implementing fit videos has to do with the tone in which the subject matter expert delivers the message.

To help you understand what I mean by tone, let's look at two examples—one good and one bad—referencing a fiberglass swimming pool.

Good:

You may be asking yourself, "Is a fiberglass pool a good fit for me?"
Great question, and it's an important one, too, as this is the type of decision you won't be able to go back on once it's in the ground. Like any type of swimming pool, fiberglass comes with a set of pros and cons.
For example, because the pool shells don't come wider than 16 feet or longer than 40 feet, there are clear size restrictions. Also, because the manufacturing process includes pre-designed "molds" to build the pool from, you can't customize a pool's shape, size, depth, etc. beyond what you see within our available models.

But if you're looking for a low-maintenance pool that's smaller than 16-by-40 feet, less than 8 feet deep—and you are able to find a shape that fits your needs—fiberglass might be a great fit for you.

Bad:

You may be asking, "Why should I consider a fiberglass pool."

Well, the reasons are obvious. They are way less maintenance, you won't have to replaster them or replace the liner, and they go in a lot faster than any other type of swimming pool.

But if you don't care about cleaning your pool all day long and want the added burdens that come with other types of swimming pools, fiberglass may not be the best fit for you.

I hope you can see the differences in the content, tone, and style of these two examples. As we've stressed many times in this book, everything comes down to trust. If it will induce more trust (because it's true), then you're on the right track. But if the tone doesn't do this (due to arrogance, dishonesty, or omission), then it's clearly not good for the business or the customer.

43

The Selling 7, Video 4

Landing Page Videos

Next to the 80 percent video, the video that often has the greatest impact from a lead generation and sales perspective is what we simply refer to as a landing page video. Without question, this simple video can have a *massive* impact on your company's bottom line.

For the purposes of this conversation, we're going to call a "landing page" any page of your site that has a form on it that someone can fill out, such as "get a quote," "contact us," "download this template," etc.

When you're online and have to fill out a form where you give someone your personal information, what emotions do you experience? At IMPACT, we've found there are four major fears people experience when giving away their information online:

- They're afraid the company will abuse their personal information (privacy).
- They're afraid they'll be spammed with multiple emails.
- They're afraid they'll be bombarded with phone calls from sales reps.
- They're simply wondering, "What will this process look like if I fill out the form?"

Therefore, a powerful key to eliminating or at least alleviating these fears is achieved by placing a video immediately next to the form that addresses each of these fears. Here's an example of how a script for this kind of video might sound:

> "OK, so you may be sitting there right now thinking to yourself, 'Should I really fill out this form? Are they going to spam me and call me to death? And what are they going to do with my information?'
>
> If you're asking yourself these questions, don't worry. Here is the exact process you'll experience with us once you enter your information…"

Once you've completed this video, you *must* put a very visible title (or call-to-action) near the video that says something to the effect of, "See exactly what will happen if you fill out this form."

Why that title? Because that's exactly what the viewer is asking, so you need to answer. And, truthfully, if you were to read a video title like that on a website, wouldn't you at least be curious to watch it? Of course, because frankness and honesty are rare online, and it's refreshing for buyers and consumers as well.

But here's what is so powerful about landing page videos: *Users will see an average conversion lift of 80 percent for that particular form if they follow these principles.*

In fact, with our clients at IMPACT, we've seen many cases where the number of people who filled out the form increased by as much as 150 percent! Think about that for a minute. How would your business be impacted if twice as many prospective buyers filled out your "get a quote" or "contact us" form over the next year?

This one video can literally generate hundreds of thousands of dollars in additional revenue per year.

Common Questions Regarding Landing Page Videos

1. **How long should they be?** Keep this video as short as possible, while still clearly addressing a prospect's concerns. Let the buyer know exactly what will happen next, as well as how and when it will happen. For most businesses, this type of video will be less than three minutes in length.

2. **What are the biggest mistakes businesses make creating landing page videos?** For the most part, businesses seem to nail the messaging of these videos, but they tend to miss the mark when it comes to drawing attention to the video off of the form. Remember, the whole point is to get the visitor to watch the video. Without that, nothing is accomplished. So include a visible, clear title and even use arrows or the like to draw attention to the video.

44

The Selling 7, Video 5

Cost and Pricing Videos

This one should be a no-brainer after reading about The Big 5 and the importance of addressing cost, but integrating video into the mix makes discussing cost and price even more effective.

Remember, the primary purpose of The Selling 7 is to move the needle for the sales team, which is why you must keep this in mind when creating a cost video. Specifically, a video on cost and pricing should:

- Address all the factors that drive the cost of a product or service up or down.
- Discuss the marketplace—why comparable products or services are cheap or expensive, and so on.
- Talk about your product or service and why it costs what it costs. (This is where you need to explain your value proposition extremely well.)

As we discussed previously, one of the great benefits of using video in the sales process is its ability to overcome communication gaps that occur when a salesperson isn't able to discuss a product or service with all decision-makers.

Now, instead of a messenger explaining to the other decision-makers what he or she heard when meeting with the salesperson, a video can explain the value of the product way better than that messenger could.

Common Questions Regarding Cost and Pricing Videos

1. **Wouldn't "How much does it cost?" just go into the 80 percent video?** You can certainly address how much something costs in an 80 percent video, but we've found that, because understanding cost is such a pivotal part of the buying process, it merits its own attention. By producing a video that dives deep into cost and value factors, you can powerfully educate a buyer and create a tremendous amount of trust in the process. Also, because their content is very specific, the video has a greater chance of doing well in search, social, and other media.

2. **How long should a cost video be?** Of all the videos in The Selling 7, this one will vary the most in length. We've helped clients produce incredibly effective cost videos that were less than two minutes, while others were longer than 10 minutes. Again, answer the cost question as thoroughly as possible.

3. **How specific should a cost video be?** We have found that specificity is almost always a good thing. For example, in the past, manufacturers wouldn't ever mention pricing because, in their minds, it would upset potential retailers or distributors. But times have changed, which is exactly why more and more manufacturers are at least including the manufacturer's suggested retail price (MSRP) on their websites, as that sets some sort of realistic expectation for the end buyer.

Having experimented with this with dozens and dozens of our clients at IMPACT, I can tell you that, almost always, the more specific a company is willing to be in answering questions about cost and pricing, the greater the increase in trust, leads, and ultimately revenue.

4. **How many cost videos should a company create?** For every major product or service that you sell, have a least one video that specifically teaches the components of cost, price, and value.

"But what if I sell hundreds of products and services?" If that's the case, start with the products or services that have (or could potentially have) the greatest impact on your company's bottom line. Then work your way down from there.

45

The Selling 7, Video 6

Customer Journey Videos

At this point in the digital age, most companies have at least some type of "social proof" on their websites, including customer quotes, testimonials, written case studies, and so on. Although these are helpful and relevant in earning buyer trust, none compare to a true "customer journey" video.

We call it the customer journey video because it's designed to follow the principle of the "hero's journey"—something that movie producers and storytellers (like Disney) have used since the beginning of time.

The traditional hero's journey has 12 parts. In the context of a customer journey video, however, this journey can be simplified into three main stages:

Stage 1: Your customer has a problem—a need, stress, worry, concern, or issue.

Stage 2: The journey is taken to fix the problem. (In most cases, this is the journey they go on with **your** company.)

Stage 3: Where they are today. They were able to fix the problem with your help. (And everyone lived happily ever after.)

The purpose of this video is for a viewer to watch it and say in his or her mind: *"They're just like me. They had the exact problem I have right now, and look how they were able to solve it."*

In other words, your viewer is literally "nodding along" in affirmation because of sympathy, empathy, and mutual understanding. Of course, you may read this and say, *"Duh, Marcus. This is common sense."*

The reality is that most companies have not produced videos like this. Fact is, the companies that do are few and far between, mainly because organizations haven't thought about them or decided they would be too difficult to get customers to agree to.

But it's our experience that, in most industries, customers are absolutely willing to make a video like this for a business, assuming that business did a great job solving their problem or addressing their needs, which makes the recording process as simple and friction-free as possible. This is, once again, why having an in-house videographer—and the flexibility that comes with that—matters so much. (But more on that later.)

Common Question Regarding Customer Journey Videos

1. **Should we have our customers sign a release when including them in a video?** Yes, absolutely. In fact, this is a best practice with employees and customers alike.

46

The Selling 7, Video 7

"Claims We Make" Videos

Every business likes to make claims about itself.

> *"We are the best _____."*
> *"We have the most _____."*
> *"No one does _____ like we do."*

Your own list of claims probably goes on and on.

When it comes to the claims we make, we generally take our clients through a powerful exercise:

- Brainstorm the claims you make as a company. (Typically, you'll find them on your website, in your sales messaging, etc.)
- Next, ask yourself, "How many of our competitors make similar, if not the same, claims as the ones we have listed?"
- Finally, ask yourself, "How many of these claims have we visually proven (through video) and not just stated?"

The activity is simple, yet it's eye-opening. Most industry "claims" are repeated over and over by competing businesses. And if everyone is making the same claims, what do they actually mean to the marketplace?

*Yep, claims such as these are just noise . . . until someone **shows** them to be true.*
You do that with a "claims we make" video.

Let's look at a specific example. One of the most popular claims businesses make around the world is, *"Our people make us different."*

Fine, fair enough. Your people are different. But what makes that true? *How am I supposed to know?*

In other words, to prove such a claim, you must show your people — their stories, their background, how they got where they are, and so on. Then others will inevitably say, *"Wow, their people really are different."*

Common Questions Regarding "Claims We Make" Videos

1. **What's the difference between a "claims we make" video and an "about us" video?** Frankly, an "about us" video, done the right way, will do exactly what a "claims we make" video does—visually prove what makes your company unique, special, and different. It will take viewers behind the scenes and allow them to get to know you on a level that makes them intuit something more genuine regarding your organization than the others they've looked at and dealt with.

That being said, most "about us" videos aren't done this way and therefore end up being a waste of time and money, as mentioned earlier.

2. **Should employees be required to participate in a "claims we make" video?** Our philosophy is that, unless the individual is in sales—therefore asking for money—don't require the employee to be on camera. That said, we do make sure they fully understand the what, how, and why of participating in this type of video and the impact it has on buyers, as well as the brand. It's funny what employees are willing to do the moment someone helps them catch the vision of "Why?"

3. **What if you don't have anything that makes you unique?** There is so much fundamentally wrong with this question, but it's one we hear often. If you're asking about this for your company, it's important to understand a couple of things:

- Just being willing to "show it"—whatever "it" is—makes you special, different, and unique.
- As businesses, because we're so entrenched in what we do, we tend to devalue the uniqueness of our product or service. Remember, if someone is buying it, it *is* interesting.

So there you have it—The Selling 7.

As you can see, there are probably more than seven videos here. In fact, if you have a full-time videographer, there's a good chance these videos will require at least a year's worth of work. But I can assure you—their impact on sales and the sales team will be dramatic.

Just remember to stay away from the fluff. Produce the videos that are proven to generate the most trust and revenue—**The Selling 7**.

47

Personalized Video for Email

A More Human Approach to Direct Digital Communication

I would be remiss if we launched the revised version of *They Ask, You Answer* without talking about an incredibly important trend that's affecting sales teams and how we use email all over the world—using personalized video.

But before we dive into the actual practice, let's pause a moment to analyze the state of sales emails for a second. Studies have shown that fewer than 20 percent of sales emails are ever opened.

That's bad. *Very* bad.

In fact, this number should be the bane of every sales manager's existence. But that's the thing about sales emails—and email in general. There are three major problems with the medium:

- First, too often, people don't open their emails.
- Second, in many cases, if they do open them, they don't actually read them.
- Finally, if someone does happen to open an email and read it, she may misunderstand its contents or the true intent behind it.

Although there is no perfect solution to these three issues, one that can certainly help overcome is the use of video, instead of text, as your means of email communication. Over the past few years, many companies—Vidyard, Wistia, and others—have produced incredibly effective, and often free, video email tools that even the most nontechnical person can learn to use within minutes.

By using these tools to create personalized video messages for use in email, you will open doors that prospects previously would not have opened. Moreover, you will become a dramatically more effective communicator in the process.

Currently, not only do sales teams within my two companies use personalized video in email every day, but creating those videos has become a part of our entire culture—from using them with our customer service team to leveraging video for internal email communication. We've also helped dozens and dozens of organizations create their own personalized videos in their email communications. If you want to harness the power of personalized video for your own company, you can do so in six easy steps.

1. Choose a Simple Technology

With more and more tools coming out every day to create video emails, make sure to choose one that is fast, easy, and immediately understood by those who aren't all that technically proficient. At IMPACT, we recommend GoVideo by Vidyard and Soapbox by Wistia. Both have free versions and can literally be learned within minutes.

2. Show Your Team Exactly How to Use It Until They're Proficient

Because most sales teams tend to be less "techie" than their marketing counterparts, it's critical you walk them through adding the software to their laptops or devices, and then show them the exact process for recording and sending videos. Generally speaking, we have found with about two hours or less of hands-on training an entire sales team can use this type of video technology proficiently.

3. Teach the Power of More Effective Subject Lines

Despite the fact that most sales professionals send out hundreds of emails a month, most have never been taught how to write a powerful subject line that makes a recipient say, *"Wow, I need to read this email."* (And yet we wonder why we have open rates of less than 20 percent.)

You and your team need to master three elements of a successful subject line:

- Personalization is absolute key. In a perfect world, not only do you mention the person's name—or company, industry, etc.—but also mention that you made the video *just for him or her.*
- Use the word "video" in your subject line. By doing so, you will automatically increase open rates.
- Identify a clear purpose for the email and reason to open it. Being specific and focused regarding your email's contents makes a significant difference.

Here is an example of a subject line my agency might use:

Mike, I Made this Video for You Re: Website Pricing

Or my swimming pool company:

John and Mary, a quick video about your swimming pool shape

Whether you plan to use video within your sales emails or not, you still should take the time to teach your sales team effective subject line strategies right away. By adhering to the three best practices for subject lines above, we've seen our clients experience an average 20- to 40-percent increase in their email open rates.

4. Learn How to Create the Perfect Thumbnail

Once your intended recipients open your email, what do they see? Hopefully, a warm and inviting face that induces immediate trust. Take the time to help your team learn how to create friendly, inviting images, including personal messages that further demonstrate the video was made specifically for someone.

5. Stick to the "Don't Stop" Rule

As we'll discuss here shortly, the quickest way to increase your team's comfort level on camera is by helping them understand the power of the "Don't Stop" rule. The more they embrace this mindset, the better they'll be at producing effective videos quickly.

6. Leaders Must Set the Tone with Their Internal Communications

We have a hard-and-fast rule at both River Pools and IMPACT:

If there is a major announcement to be made to the team, it's only to be done with video. Never text.

Why? First, there are the obvious reasons we've already covered, but I want to bring two others to your attention within the context of leadership using personalized video:

First, you'll receive significantly fewer questions from your team if you share an announcement via personalized video than you might have if you had shared it in an all-text email. By watching a video, your team will more fully understand what has been presented. Video is not perfect, of course, but it is a much more clear and concrete way of communicating than text.

Second, you want to show your team that you "eat your own dog food." In this crazy digital world, it's critical we as leaders capitalize on opportunities to humanize our businesses and create company cultures where people actually know and appreciate each other. Without question, video is more capable of doing this than text messages bouncing back and forth all day long. Plus, if we're going to ask employees to communicate in a different way, shouldn't we be the first to set the example?

Although we're still in the early days of video emails becoming mainstream around the world, within a few short years, this type of communication will become the standard. Wild as that may sound, consider how much more clear and efficient your communication will be through personalized video. Video humanizes what is often a soulless method of communication, so it only makes sense that we embrace it as a better way of communicating today.

48

How to Hire an In-House Videographer

Let's assume you feel video—and "showing it"—are fundamental to your business going forward. If you do want to become a "media company" and produce great, impactful content like The Selling 7, how are you going to do it?

You must embrace two important realities:

- Someone must "own" your video production in-house—a videographer.
- Your team must clearly understand the what, how, and why of video, while also being willing to learn how to communicate on camera effectively.

Your immediate reaction upon reading this is very likely the same as so many business owners and managers have said to me over the past few years when I've spoken on this subject: *"Why would a business like mine ever have the need for a full-time videographer? Are there really 40 hours of work per week for such a position in my niche?"*

To answer the first question, let's just go back to The Selling 7. Videos, when done well, are likely going to take a videographer months and months to produce.

Let's look at it another way. My agency, IMPACT, has worked hand-in-hand with organizations across a wide range of industries with video, and never have we seen a situation when we said, "You know, there simply isn't enough work here for a videographer to work full-time."

Besides that, if you truly understand the incredible importance the videographer position will have on your sales and marketing numbers, you would never question whether or not this should be a full-time position.

With all the successful customers we've worked with, we've never, after the first year of doing video, had anyone question the need for this position. Rather, most are debating, "Should we hire another?"

The last argument I'll make for the videographer before discussing what to look for in this person is this: *In 10 years, the position "videographer" will be just as important and prominent to an organization's success as a "sales manager" is today.*

You might be thinking to yourself, "No way, Marcus. You're crazy." But it's true. Today, most organizations see the position of "sales manager" as critical and important to their success. The same will be true for videographers in the very near future—as their financial impact from a sales perspective will often be more significant than that of a sales manager.

OK, now that we've discussed the need to hire a videographer, let's look at exactly "how" you can find the perfect person to lead the video production efforts for your organization going forward. Because this position can and will have such a massive impact on your success, it's not something you'll want to rush or take lightly. Doing it right the first time will be well worth it in the long run.

At IMPACT, we have assisted well over 100 clients in their search for a videographer. As you might imagine, we've made some great hires and also seen our share of complete duds.

Zach Basner, IMPACT's director of video training and strategy, has led our efforts in growing the educational video department of the agency and has found the following to be essential to this process.

Identifying Personality Traits of a Videographer

The person who fills this position will be the visual storyteller of the company. As such, he needs to be a *great* fit for the culture of your business. He will have frequent contact with other employees and, in certain scenarios, will have to give and receive criticism to develop the best content.

Somebody who is uncomfortable, overly introverted, or doesn't mesh well with the company culture you've established won't succeed in this role. It's also important to look for a strong desire for personal growth. Each video she creates will, we hope, be better than the last, so you really want your videographer to take feedback well. Also, because video technology is evolving at such a rapid rate, the desire for personal development and continual learning is absolutely essential.

Also, consider this — the videographer is probably going to be the only employee (or one of a select few) who focuses on video, so he or she can't rely on a manager or colleague to help when it comes to the technicalities of video production.

During the interview process, focus heavily on seeking out the following traits:

- Able to work with a team or on their own.
- Own the production process and do what it takes to make great content.
- Self-starting and treat the brand as if it were their own.
- Deal well with constructive criticism and are able to receive feedback easily.
- Have great communication skills and are able to interview and make people comfortable.
- Energetic and able to excite others on the team to be on camera.
- Look at the content from the eye of the viewer to create the best experience.
- Lifelong learners and eager to identify new learning opportunities.

More often than not, assuming they have the video production skills, someone who is fun and energetic is going to be a great candidate for this role.

Because many people within your organization might not particularly enjoy being in front of a camera (especially at first), their ability to inspire others is arguably as important as their ability to use the camera.

What a Good Videographer Candidate Should Demonstrate

A common question businesses ask is, "Should our candidate have earned a degree in video production or something comparable?" Although having a degree is generally a great sign, don't see it as a moral imperative. Especially with the proliferation of video production experience within today's younger generation, it's not unusual to see phenomenal content that has almost no "formal" training behind it.

Remember, this is a "creative" position. Ultimately, the person's practical skills will make all the difference. Here is a quick list our company uses that should guide you in the proper direction for a hire:

Potential Fields of Study

- Journalism
- Education
- Video production
- Graphic design
- Photography

Technical Skills

- Proficient with video editing software (Adobe Premiere or Final Cut Pro are the most common)
- Experience with Adobe After Effects or Motion
- Experience with Adobe Photoshop and Adobe Illustrator is a plus
- Can conduct research and purchase needed equipment
- Can operate and maintain proper levels and calibration of cameras, audio and video recorders, and other production equipment
- Embraces new technology, such as augmented reality (AR), virtual reality (VR), etc., as it happens
- Understands the importance of tracking video marketing metrics

Creative Skills

- Proficient at storyboarding, scripting, and conceptualizing
- Understands basic and advanced composition techniques
- Understands the fundamentals of branding
- Detail-oriented and able to identify quality issues in audio and video others might miss
- Understands the basics of social media platforms, native social video, and content promotion through social channels

Video Portfolio

- Has a YouTube, Instagram, or Vimeo channel
- Has a personal website with a portfolio

These are just some ideas of how to gauge experience and skill level. However, know that not all videographer candidates are going to meet all of the criteria. Remember—your candidate must display traits that lend themselves to business storytelling and not just cinematic knowledge.

Granted, this can be trained and taught, but don't lose sight of the fact that just because someone is good at "making videos" doesn't mean he or she is skilled at the art of producing *sales and marketing* videos.

Extra Interview Questions for Your Videographer Candidates

If your candidate has already passed the company culture fit screening, has the technical and creative skills required, and is equipped with a stellar video portfolio, you're on track.

Here are a few more questions you can ask during the interview and throughout the hiring process that will yield valuable insights into candidates' capabilities as a videographer, as well as how successful they'll be at your company:

- What's your favorite part of video editing? What is your least favorite?
- What websites or resources do you use to learn new strategies and techniques and improve your skills?
- What don't you like about the video production process?
- What are the most important steps in pre-production?
- Tell me about a time when your footage didn't turn out as you had hoped. What did you learn? How did you fix it?
- Who are some of your favorite videographers, channels, or influencers? *(If they don't have any, this could be a sign they don't love learning.)*
- What makes a perfect visual story?
- What videos have you seen online that were poorly done?
- When you see someone doing something wrong on camera, how do you generally offer feedback? Can you provide specific examples of those instances?
- How, specifically, do you deal with someone who doesn't feel comfortable on camera?
- What's the toughest piece of feedback or criticism you've ever received for some of your work? Was it valid? (Self-awareness is essential for this position.)

- In your opinion, what makes a business video different from, say, a short film?
- From what you know about our company so far, what's an important element of telling our story that's missing?
- What do you feel are the most important videos our company could produce right now?

As you can see, it's important that you find out how knowledgeable they are, how well they receive feedback, and if they're up for the challenge of making amazing videos for your organization. Once you've vetted your candidates, it's time for the practical challenge.

A Simple Video Assignment as Part of the Interview Process

What videographer interview would be complete without seeing what the candidate is capable of? That's where the practical video assignment comes in.

By this point, your candidate has probably "talked the talk" during the interview process but now let's see whether he or she can "walk the walk" by actually creating a video to your specifications.

This assignment not only shows you the candidate's video skills, but also tells you a lot about the person's time management, creativity, critical thinking, and communication skills.

Here's what you should have them do:

- **Have your candidates make a video explaining why they want the job.** This will give you an idea of how effective they are at telling a story. Also, how they present themselves could give you an idea of how well they understand your brand.
- **Give a certain timeframe to complete the video—between two and five days.** This shows how well they perform under a time constraint, how fast they are able to turn content around, and how creative they can be under pressure.
- **Have them develop a script or storyboard to accompany the video.** This shows their creative process beyond the cameras and lights. Many times this is what they'll be presenting when they start a new project. How prepared can they be?
- **Allow them to be creative and think outside the scope of a traditional marketing video.** Let them know that they are free to tell the story as they wish to tell it, so to be creative and have fun with it.

There you have it. When hiring a videographer for your company, don't skip any of the steps. And please, don't see your organization as the exception.

*We know that we must **show** it, and not just **say** it.*

A full-time videographer working hand-in-hand with the rest of your team can very well make this possible.

49

Team Buy-In on Video, Performance Tips, and Long-Term Success

Now that we've established our goal to become a media company, are embracing The Selling 7, and have found the right videographer—we still have one major obstacle in front of us: *engaging our team and gaining their buy-in on video.*

As we discussed earlier, so much of digital sales and marketing success starts with a basic understanding of the what, how, and why of video. Only when that understanding exists can video become a culture of who you are, allowing you to achieve your greatest potential.

Over the past few years, I've been shocked at how many companies have approached me and said: *"Marcus, we tried video. But after we hired a video production company and attempted to produce these videos, we realized some-thing—we're just not good on camera."*

Alas, the "we're just not good on camera" mindset strikes again.

I've traveled the globe speaking to audiences about sales and marketing and this may be the number 1 excuse I hear from audience members push-ing back on video—other than the claim "but my business is different."

But think of it this way—what would members of your sales team say if you asked them, *"Are you good with people?"* If they are like 99 percent of the sales professionals I've spoken to, they'd immediately pipe up and say, *"Oh yes, I'm very good with people."*

Think about that for a second. Why is it that most of us would say we're good with people yet terrible on camera?

It's simply not possible, which is why the moment you and your co-workers start seeing the camera as a person—yes, I mean that—and not as a camera, everything starts to change.

I have personally witnessed this phenomenon again and again. Over the past few years, I've spent hours training sales teams and other subject matter experts how to be effective on camera. With a few tips and techniques—and a little practice—it truly is remarkable how quickly one can become not just comfortable, but also effective, on camera.

While we can't present an exhaustive analysis of on-camera performance in this book, I want to give you enough to begin with your team, the three most fundamental rules of on-camera success. If you commit to following these three rules and make them a part of your company culture, you'll be amazed at how quickly your team starts to perform and communicate effectively on camera.

1. Don't Stop

Have you ever watched live TV weather reporters "just keep going" in the middle of a hurricane or storm? Ever wondered how they do it? Well, for the most part, they have one simple rule: *You can't stop, no matter what.*

This is what makes live TV special.

The same holds true when you shoot video with your team. Your people need to understand that, regardless of what they say or how they say it, they must simply "keep going"—no matter what.

This is true due to three realities:

- The moment people know they can stop while being recorded is the moment they will start stopping a lot more.
- Most mistakes we make on camera can be fixed by a videographer in post-production.

- By moving forward and finishing, you "work out the kinks" in what you're attempting to say—like writing a first draft to an article—allowing it to be said better the second time.

The "don't stop" rule is something your sales team has followed for years. For example, when was the last time one of them was on a sales call with a prospect or customer and suddenly said, "Oops, I messed up what I was trying to say. Let's just start the whole conversation over again"?

Yep, sales professionals learn early on that they must keep going, regardless of what happens or what is said in the moment. This exact same mindset should be applied to video communication as well.

2. But You Can Do It Again

Although we don't want to stop in the middle of a take or segment, it is absolutely fine to do it again once it's finished. Often, because we're "working it out"—figuring out what we're trying to say—with the first take, the way we deliver the message may not be as fluid or incisive as we would like it to be.

It's surprising just how well we will say something on the second try—bigger smile, more concise, greater clarity—assuming we continue to follow the "don't stop" rule.

This being said, if you're following these rules but still need more than three or four attempts to "say it right," then there is a good chance you should move on to another video—one you're more comfortable and familiar with.

I'll offer two other suggestions before we move on from on-camera performance.

3. The 3-Second Smile

A wise man once said, "By small and simple things are great things brought to pass." The same is true with video communication—particularly when it comes to the magic of the smile. Yes, the smile.

"OK, Marcus. I already know it's important to smile."

I know you know this, but the reality is most people forget this the moment the camera's red recording light comes on.

The specific technique we teach at IMPACT is so simple you may be tempted to disregard it. But don't, because it works.

Here it is: ***Start smiling three seconds before hitting the record button.***

Yes, three seconds.

Why?

First, because once the video starts, you want to be coming off of your smile, not going into it. This establishes an immediate tone of being warm, friendly, and trustworthy.

Second, it's much harder to be nervous when you're smiling than when you're not. If you don't believe me, try. It works.

Therefore, make smiling a major habit with your team. Practice the three-second smile rule with every video and the results will follow.

The Problem with Scripts

One of the questions I'm asked most by companies attempting to integrate video into their culture is whether or not they should be using scripts. To answer this question, think of it this way: When was the last time one of your sales team members was on a sales call and, after being asked a question by a prospect, said, "Hmm, good question, let me pull out my script and read you the answer"?

It very likely has never happened.

If sales professionals don't use scripts when they're face-to-face with prospects or customers, why would they use them on videos? Plus, the moment you (as a viewer) watch a video and realize someone is reading from a script is the moment you start to lose trust in that person and doubt his or her subject matter expertise.

Each person on your team is an expert in some way, shape, or form. They are all used to answering questions. In fact, many have answered thousands over the years. So allow them to talk to the camera exactly as they would with a prospect.

Does this mean you don't have some type of potential order or even a rudimentary outline sketched out for the video? No, it does not. But it does mean that you focus more on being as real and human as possible, rather than on presenting your message in such a rote and robotic manner.

Getting Buy-In and "Embracing the Messy"

As I said earlier in this book, do not make the mistake of bringing in a video production company and just "throwing" your team on camera. This strategy, without question, will do more harm than good. Just as with everything else we've discussed, your people must understand the what, how, and why of video. They need on-camera performance training.

Does this take much time?

No, definitely not.

Frankly, everything we've discussed about video can be covered in one day with your team. We've led well over 100 workshops on video and have found that they do not need to be nearly as complex as some people believe.

What does take time, though, is for people to have the willingness to "embrace the messy" that comes with creating a culture of video. Like anything else that really matters in business, there is a learning curve here. It's going to be clunky.

Not all videos will come out as you hoped.

Not everyone is going to be great on camera the first day.

Not every video will take off as anticipated.

But it will be worth it.

So embrace the messy. Get through the learning curve, and when you come out on the other side, you'll ultimately humanize and add soul to your business in a way you never realized would be possible. Having worked with so many companies on this, I know this is true. You, too, will experience it for yourself.

"But I'm just not good on camera."

Before we close the book on the topic of video, there is one last story I want to share that represents everything we've spoken about.

I was once hired by a real estate company to train their agents on how to better communicate on camera. To do the training, we brought my video team to a high-end property they were attempting to sell. We decided to record videos showing the different areas of the estate, thereby killing two birds with one stone—performance training and marketing videos.

After I explained the two fundamental rules of video performance to their team, we went down to a lake on the property and planned to have one of the agents (we'll call her Jane) explain the different features of the lake on camera. Less than 30 seconds into the recording, Jane stopped what she was saying and said, "Darn, I messed this up. Can I just start again?"

My response was swift and frank, as it always is in these situations: *"Jane, our rule is simple. Don't stop. No matter what. I know this may sound odd or uncomfortable for you right now, but you must trust me here. So this time, keep going, and do not stop."*

Jane's response was typical: ***"But you don't understand, Marcus. I'm just not good on camera."***

Again, I replied, *"That's fine, Jane—but this time, don't stop."*

She agreed and we then proceeded with the video. Although it wasn't perfect in her eyes, she got through it.

Over the next hour, we continued recording videos of different areas of the estate, with Jane being the main agent on camera. After about an hour of doing this, we went through a section where Jane completed three straight videos, each taking only one attempt.

She was on a roll.

Suddenly, she looked at me with a big smile and said, *"Marcus, I think I may be a natural!"*

50

Case Study 6

How a Lifting and Rigging Company Became the Ultimate Example of They Ask, You Answer Success and Culture

A few years ago, I traveled to Cleveland to give a talk to a small group of CEOs. Mazzella Companies CEO Tony Mazzella was one of them. Mazzella Companies is one of the largest independently owned companies in the lifting, overhead crane, and rigging space, employing more than 700 people in 30 locations spanning North America. Beneath the Mazzella umbrella are several lifting, rigging, and material-handling companies, as well as a few prominent businesses in the architectural metals market.

Following that event, Tony came on as a client: *"Listening to Marcus speak about his They Ask, You Answer philosophy, I remember thinking, 'Wow, this is what I've felt was always missing.'"*

Mazzella's Initial Approach to They Ask, You Answer

Tony felt confident the principles of They Ask, You Answer would allow them to overcome their most pressing marketing and sales challenges, so he took action quickly: *"I felt a lot of excitement talking with Marcus and decided to initiate They Ask, You Answer right away. We hired a content manager and videographer within a few weeks and started training with Marcus and IMPACT in June 2017."*

Although Tony is not someone who "dabbles" in anything—he commits fully to something, when he knows that's how he's going to achieve success—he did limit the company's initial focus to the lifting and rigging side of the business until he saw the results he was looking for.

Their Commitment Began to Pay Off

Within a few months of making that commitment to being the best teachers in their industry—producing between two and three articles as well as at least two videos per week—the incredible results started rolling in for Mazzella.

When Mazzella first began publishing content, their website was getting around 5,500 visits per month and was ranking for 2,683 keywords with 174 of those keywords ranking on the first page. At the time, they also had almost no presence on YouTube.

By focusing on The Big 5, the team at Mazzella quickly found their content ranking on the first page of search results. In fact, so few of their competitors were creating content for their industry that one of the first articles they ever published—"How Much Does an Overhead Crane Cost?"—ranked number 1 for the relevant keyword on Google within a week's time.

By creating high-quality content that answered the most pressing questions of their buyers, Mazzella was able to stand out in an industry of "ostriches."

By October of the same year—only months into their journey with They Ask, You Answer—they began to see more substantive, far-reaching results. Their website traffic had jumped by 27 percent, and they also saw significant gains in lead generation.

Upon seeing what was possible, Tony scaled up their commitment to They Ask, You Answer. He hired another full-time content manager and videographer, with the direction to go "full steam ahead" with Mazzella's architectural metals division, Sheffield Metals.

Mazzella's Success Came Down to Hiring the Right People

We've talked about it already, but the team at Mazzella was able to accomplish so much so early on because they understood how important it was to have the right people on their team right away. When I talk about the importance of hiring the "right people," however, I'm not saying you need to hire the most knowledgeable subject matter experts in a given field to produce your content.

Sometimes that does work out, but—for the most part—you should focus on finding folks who possess the writing and video production skills you don't already have in-house. Time and again, we see that the best people to fill those critical content manager and videographer seats are those who are trained in journalism and videography. The industry knowledge will come naturally over time as they start to interview and perform research to create the content you need.

Using Mazzella as an example, all four of their key content contributors had no prior experience in that industry. What they brought to the table was their expertise in extracting the information they needed from Mazzella's subject matter experts and translating it into quality, engaging content.

Mazzella's content manager, Mike Close, reflected, "When we started producing content, we started with the basics. We had a '101' mentality. Since we were new to the company and the industry ourselves, we decided to start with content that answers the basic questions: What is an overhead crane? What are the different types of overhead cranes? What happens during an inspection? Etc."

Mike brings up a great point here—often, your experts are almost too knowledgeable about the products and services they sell to create effective content around it for your potential buyers. Even with the best intentions, they'll gloss over basic fundamentals and the core questions buyers are asking early in the purchasing process.

Mazzella's content specialist, Julianne Calapa, agreed with Mike: "I didn't come from a metal roofing background," Calapa noted. "In fact, I knew nothing about metal roofs. But through spending time with our salespeople and interviewing industry experts, I've become one of the metal roofing experts for the industry. My name is attached to all the metal roofing articles being read online."

Again, one of the key determining factors in Mazzella's success with They Ask, You Answer was their investment in hiring the right people from the beginning—*and everyone from their team agrees.*

Sheffield Metals VP of Sales and Marketing Adam Mazzella commented, "Company growth is a byproduct of the individual's growth and the team's growth. We would not be where we are today without hiring the best people."

Why Insourcing Outperforms Outsourcing Every Time

Like most companies starting out with They Ask, You Answer, Mazzella had to decide whether to produce their own content or outsource, as so many others tend to do. After some consideration, they saw greater value in keeping their content creation efforts in-house.

"Having someone on your team dedicated to producing content is invaluable. Many people work with agencies or outsource their content to freelancers. These people are never *really* going to understand your brand, your products, or services," Mike told me. "Why would you not want someone fully invested in what you've built?" He continued, "When you've got someone on-hand to create your content, you have someone available 24 hours a day, seven days a week. Someone who can jump into a meeting to take notes, to pick up and go on-site for a project to shoot video. Having those resources in-house is the most invaluable part of success."

Sheffield Metals' Thad Barnette shared Mike's sentiment: "The amount of videos we've shot over the past year would be nearly impossible to get that volume from an outsourced video agency. The amount of time we spend with the sales team, leadership team, and going to industry trade shows would be unthinkable to have a video agency do."

There Are No Silos at Mazzella

I talk a lot about how to dismantle the silos between sales and marketing—both in this book and as a speaker—because you can't implement They Ask, You Answer successfully for your company without doing so.

Few companies understand this as well as Mazzella. From total leadership buy-in on their new business philosophy to the joint effort from both sales and marketing, the team at Mazzella fully embraced They Ask, You Answer as a culture, rather than a set of marketing tactics.

"Tony gives [the marketing team] a lot of leeway to do what we think is right for the company," Marketing Manager Michael Minissale shared. "All good CEOs push their people. Tony knows how to push and what to push. He knows better than we do what he can get out of people."

At Mazzella, the sales team doesn't just chase the leads marketing brings in—they help pitch the topics the marketing team develops content around as well as use the content in their sales process. Through working with their videographers, the sales team have become accustomed to using video in their day-to-day selling.

"We use what we call 'digital handshakes' for the salespeople to use in one-to-one emails," Thad explained. "Our salespeople have shot over 150 of these types of videos alone."

These digital handshakes are short, custom videos the sales team shoots on their own introducing themselves via video to new prospects. So before a salesperson ever meets or speaks with a prospect in person, that prospect already knows what the salesperson looks and sounds like, and has a preview of who he or she is as a person. It's a much more powerful way of making an introduction during the sales process.

Not all are comfortable on camera the first time they step in front of one, however. It can take some time adjusting to talking to a blinking red light as if it's a real person.

Mazzella had a clever way of making their sales team familiar with using camera equipment as well as being on camera. After meeting with their marketing and sales teams about their goals with video, each member of the sales staff was issued a GoPro-like camera.

Videographer Devon McCarty explains, "The thought behind it was to familiarize our staff with shooting their own videos and getting comfortable being on camera. We encouraged them to first take the cameras home and just shoot whatever they liked." As they became more comfortable, members of the sales team were asked to start using those cameras for work—filming videos of products, capturing client testimonials, and so on.

Not only did Mazzella's video team see those desired comfort levels with video rise in sales, but they also had a new pipeline of relevant, useful video content they could use in the creation of educational videos.

Educating Customers, Employees, and Entire Industries

If you look closely at all of the companies we've featured as case studies in this book, you should see they all share the three fundamental characteristics required for success with They Ask, You Answer: buy-in from their leadership, active collaboration between their sales and marketing teams, and a shared mission to become the best educators for their buyers in their chosen field or industry.

But it's worth noting that the team at Mazzella has set an example for other companies in the way they've scaled their commitment to They Ask, You Answer. By starting with a "101" approach to their marketing efforts in the first year, they realized they could be doing more with their content than just answering questions in blog articles or longer pieces of premium content, such as downloadable guides or ebooks.

In fact, once they took a look back at what they had done, they realized they laid the foundation for a robust educational program.

"By the second year, we had covered the 101s and had a ton of content spread all over," Mike shared. "We realized we had created enough material to not just put out a couple of ebooks, but that we could combine those materials into an online course that was something unique to our industry." He continued, "We came up with the 'overhead crane buying course' for somebody who had never purchased an overhead crane before. We took our articles, videos, and ebooks and put everything into one curriculum that takes people on an easy-to-follow path. The course helps people through everything from putting their budgets together, getting bids on the project, to the design and fabrication process."

The beauty of what Mazzella achieved with this course, however, is that it's no longer just for the benefit of their potential buyers and customers. Now the entire staff is required to complete the course.

According to Adam, "The course has really helped make our message consistent both externally for our customers and internally for our staff. All of our staff knows exactly what conversations to have with each type of customer and how we can educate those customers with our content. It's not a strict marketing message; it's galvanized our sales team."

Thad says their online course materials and their educational YouTube channels—the latter of which have garnered more than 130,000 views as of this writing—have also caught the attention of others in their industry: "Since we started creating video content, every trade show I've gone to since launching our Metal Roofing YouTube Channel, people come up to me and say, 'Hey, you're that metal roofing guy from YouTube,' and they take selfies with me and tell me how much they appreciate the content."

"We were down at an international trade show, and one of our sales guys told us he was at the booth when a guy approached him and said, 'Hey, I know who your company is,'" recalls VP of Marketing Bill Franz. "When the sales guy asked the gentleman if he had any questions or needed a demo, the guys responded, 'No, I went online and checked you out. I've read a lot of your blogs. I've seen a lot of your videos. From those materials, I know what your machine does, I know what product is right for me, and I'll be back tomorrow to buy my equipment.' For us, that was total validation for everything we've been doing with inbound marketing."

On top of that, well-respected, major industry publications have used Mazzella's content. "One of the things I'm most proud of is that we've had four major industry publishers reach out to us to use our content in their print publications," Mike recalled. "It's the highest compliment you can receive when your peers in the industry find what you're creating as valuable to their audience."

The Results

In addition to a 600 percent increase in website traffic and a 650 percent increase in leads generated on a monthly basis, Adam explained that Mazzella's commitment to the principles of They Ask, You Answer has also resulted in remarkable revenue growth for the business:

"In the 18 months since starting They Ask, You Answer as our company's philosophy, *our sales revenues are up by almost $20 million.* We attribute They Ask, You Answer as the primary methodology for how we're driving our marketing, which then translates to how we're driving our sales process."

As for Tony, he is humble in the framing of his company's successes with They Ask, You Answer: "Being able to share our knowledge and expertise with our industry and get the recognition as a thought leader, that's the greatest achievement. Overall, it's been a tremendous morale boost to the sales team, marketing team, and the company in general."

PART V

How to Build the Perfect They Ask, You Answer Website

Since the first edition of *They Ask, You Answer* was released, one of the most consistent questions we've received has been:

"How do we apply the principles of this book to our company's website design and layout?"

Although what's possible with website design is always evolving, it is my hope that this section will at least crystalize some of the more practical "evergreen" ways you can transform your website based on the They Ask, You Answer philosophy.

First, we talk about two major shifts in buying behavior that have heavily influenced how we should be looking at the functionality of our websites—real-time conversations and self-selection tools.

Following that, we review the seven aspects of your website's design and user experience you should evaluate and improve, as needed. By doing so, you will position yourself at the digital forefront of your industry.

51 | Real-Time Conversations Are Changing How They're Asking and We're Answering

We've spent much of this book talking about how buyer behavior has changed—specifically, your buyers are now firing up their search engines of choice in pursuit of expert advice, information, answers, and solutions when making a purchasing decision.

But another dramatic shift in buyer behavior has occurred since I sat down and wrote the first edition of *They Ask, You Answer*. In order to understand what's changed, however, I want to ask you a question that HubSpot VP of Marketing Jon Dick asked me during a recent conversation: *"When was the last time you actually communicated with any of your close friends over email as a way of exchanging information or planning something?"*

After a few moments of silence, I shook my head and laughed a little bit.

"You know, Jon," I said, "I don't know. Longer than I would probably care to admit."

That was precisely his point.

The Way We Communicate Has Fundamentally Changed

Think about it—today, we live so much of our lives online. We've got Facebook, Instagram, Twitter, Reddit, WhatsApp, Snapchat, native text messaging, and countless other applications at our fingertips that not only enable us to share our lives with the world, but also empower us to communicate in much smaller group messaging settings with our friends, family, and loved ones.

All in real time.

What's more, we live in a time when our smartphones are like an extension of our persons.

In fact, Tech Times found that more than 46 percent of Americans check their smartphones before getting out of bed, and almost 30 percent of people surveyed by The Boston Consulting Group said they'd give up seeing their friends in person before giving up their smartphones.

We've moved away from our desktops, phone calls, voicemails, antiquated chat rooms, and the meandering, tell-all emails of yesteryear. Now, instead of corresponding—or even picking up the phone—we look to the internet not only as our platform for finding information, but also for having *conversations*.

What does this have to do with your buyers? *Everything.*

We all now have this built-in expectation that communicating online should be easy, painless, and immediate, right? But that expectation now extends beyond our private lives. We now expect to be able to ask questions of companies about their products and services online, and have that same real-time, conversational experience we have when we're asking our spouses, partners, and friends, *"Hey, what's the plan for dinner tonight?"*

More to the point, your buyers are still asking questions and wanting you to provide them with thorough, sincerely helpful answers, but now, there's a new twist. They're asking you questions *right now*. And they want you to answer *immediately*.

This new consumer expectation has given rise to something marketers call "conversational marketing."

What Is Conversational Marketing and Where Did It Come From?

Conversational marketing refers to the one-to-one conversations buyers have with brands across different channels, whether that's through live chat, chatbots, Facebook Messenger, Slack, text, and so on.

That's why, at IMPACT, we refer to this concept more directly and simply as having "real-time conversations" with anyone who wants to talk to us—whether they're potential buyers with questions about our services or someone who has a more general, tactical question about digital marketing.

Conversational marketing is another example of how brands and companies are being challenged to continually meet their customers where they live—in a digital sense—as our relationship with the internet continues to evolve.

At its core, conversational marketing is everything They Ask, You Answer is supposed to be.

It's all about making the whole buyer experience of getting answers to questions and, ultimately, making purchases as effortless and friction-free as possible.

And that's *exactly* what you need to be doing.

"Customers have all the power in the buying process," says Dave Gerdhardt, who is the VP of marketing at Drift, a conversational marketing platform for businesses. "As a result, whichever company makes it easier to buy is going to win. That's how we make decisions, today, as consumers."

But this trend isn't new, according to Dave—and he's absolutely right. Just look at what happened to Blockbuster. After its founding in 1985, Blockbuster dominated the at-home video rental market for more than a decade. Then, in 1997, a company called Netflix saw an opportunity with DVDs, where movie lovers wouldn't have to leave their homes to rent their favorite flicks.

It wasn't long before consumers were forgoing trips to Blockbuster—and all of those awful late fees. Instead, they enjoyed the convenience of renting DVDs through an online queue and having them delivered to their doorstep a few short days later. Once they were finished, they could put those watched movies in prepaid envelopes, drop them in the mailbox, and then wait for their next movies to arrive.

All without ever talking to a person face-to-face or having to go to a store.

As a result, by 2005, Blockbuster had lost 75 percent of its market value and...well, we all know what happened next.

You Can't Dictate the Buying Process

"That's the biggest mistake companies like Blockbuster make," Dave told me. "If you try to dictate the buying process for customers, you will fail. So that's what we think about a lot with conversational marketing. It goes beyond the technology. It's about being there for potential customers 24 hours a day, seven days a week, 365 days a year. Because that's how they expect you to be there for them."

For example, Jon's work with HubSpot takes him all around the world. But, as we all know, preparing for a trip can be hectic, which means that sometimes details slip through the cracks—even for the best planners. So, occasionally, Jon will find himself, carry-on and smartphone in-hand, about to board a flight to a distant country when he remembers that he has yet to add a temporary international data plan through his carrier, AT&T.

If this had been five or 10 years ago, Jon probably would have had to call AT&T's customer service line and wait on hold for 15 to 20 minutes before speaking to a human being who could solve his problem.

Now, it's a completely different story.

"I've actually found that AT&T's in-app chat makes adding a temporary international data plan quick and painless," Jon says. "I literally can just chat them and say, 'Hey, I'm about to travel, can you add a 1GB *Passport* to my account?'"

In under five minutes, without ever having to talk to someone, it's done.

Now, you're probably saying to yourself, *"I get what you're saying, Marcus. I really do. I don't want to lose deals to my competitors, but how does a company of my size adapt to such a massive change? Where do I even start?"*

Those are the exact questions we are going to answer together on the following pages. There are simple strategies you can implement and basic steps you can take right now that will immediately empower you to embrace conversational marketing in a way that makes you irresistible to your buyers and helps you stand out from your competitors.

But before we talk about those tactics, I want to stress that it's of the utmost important that you *do not skim* through what comes in the rest of this chapter. While your application of conversational marketing will be unique to your company's size, goals, industry, and so on, you must understand one thing: Unless your organization is never asked questions by anyone, ever—which, let's be honest, is highly unlikely—you will eventually need to embrace the notion of being conversational online in some form or another.

There is no sign or symptom within your company you need to look for that will indicate it's time to start with conversational marketing.

Either you want to answer your customers' questions—in real time, as they ask them—or you do not.

How to Start Conversational Marketing for Your Business

You need to do two things to get started with real-time conversations. First, you need to shift your mindset about how you communicate with your potential buyers online through these new channels. Second, you need to learn the tactics associated with using conversational technology to connect with potential buyers.

Adopt a Truly "Conversational" Mindset

Let's say you text a friend of yours, "Hey, I haven't heard from you in a while—are we OK?" Then, for the next five to 10 minutes, you see those bubbles appearing and disappearing, indicating that your friend is writing a response, pausing, and then rewriting portions of the reply.

As you await an answer, you're probably thinking, "Come on! Just say something! **Anything!**"

It's frustrating, right?

That's why, before you turn on any sort of conversational channel for your company, you need to understand that your buyers will have the same feelings of frustration if you take a long time to send responses to their questions. In these conversations, you need to chat in a more fragmented way—the way you might communicate with a friend—so your buyers feel immediate gratification and aren't left wondering, "What the heck is taking them so long to respond to me?"

In short, you need to shift your mindset to a more informal way of communicating. The way you succeed with conversational marketing is by being conversational and human. Save the thoughtful paragraphs for your email newsletters, blog articles, and landing pages.

Start Small and Test

No matter what conversational technology you decide to use, the process for starting is actually quite easy:

- First, identify your "high-intent" pages on your website—contact us pages, "get started" or demo request landing pages, etc.
- Then, add a chatbot or live chat functionality to a select number of pages—even just one—and see how your website visitors respond.

When HubSpot added more real-time options to their contact page—including a chat option (therefore giving them the ability to address concerns and questions the very moment someone is on that page)—they saw a 160 percent increase in conversions on that page.

Can you imagine what kind of impact it would have on your business if you could almost double the number of people raising their hands to say, *"I want to have a conversation with you,"* all because you made it easier for people to do so on their terms?

At IMPACT, we've seen countless chats come through every single day, ever since we started using conversational tools on our website. Many of those casual conversations quickly transformed into closed deals—some of which likely never would have happened had the conversation not occurred in the moment.

Explore New Conversational Opportunities

Once you're ready to scale up, add conversational opportunities for your buyers on FAQ or knowledge base–type site pages—if someone has come to that type of page, it's very likely he or she has done so because of a problem or question, so facilitating conversations with your buyers on those pages is a fantastic way for you to offer solutions and answers in real time.

You can also explore how you're presenting content to people. For example, what if you flipped the traditional process of a visitor converting on a form to gain access to a piece of premium content on a landing page on its head?

Instead, you could create a chatbot that asks if someone would like a downloadable copy of a piece of content. If someone says yes, that file could be transmitted through that chat window in a matter of seconds, creating a more helpful and positive experience for someone visiting your site.

HubSpot has seen a lot of success with an SEO quiz bot they created specifically for Facebook Messenger designed to take the place of their more standard eight-field landing page form for a gated piece of content. They published a video on Facebook about SEO myths, but in the caption of the video, the HubSpot team wrote:

"Think you're an SEO master? Type 'SEO' in our comments to play our SEO Quiz in Messenger to find out your score."

Once users took the quiz, they would receive a personalized score based on their responses, as well as an invitation to explore a more in-depth piece of premium content about SEO strategy.

Your Questions Answered About Conversational Marketing

Although some of the conversational technologies we've discussed in this chapters—for example, live chat—aren't exactly revolutionary, the business application of real-time conversational tactics as a way of communicating with buyers is still quite new for a lot of companies.

To help you get started, I've provided the answers to a few of the most common questions we've been asked about how businesses can see the best results from facilitating real-time conversations.

1. **What are some of the most common mistakes companies make with conversational marketing?** In our experience, the companies that fail in their conversational efforts—whether they're B2B or B2C—are those that approach it with an expectation that they'll still see drastically different results even though they're unwilling to change what they're doing right now.

This can manifest itself in a few different ways:

- They build an exact replica of what currently happens on a form, landing page, or email in a conversational interface, without making any changes that take into account it being a real-time conversation that should feel human.
- If they're using live chat on their site, they let their potential buyers wait too long to get a response while they try to craft perfect answers. They don't adapt their communication style to be more in line with the "instant messaging" back-and-forth expectations of today.
- Their goal with conversational marketing is to cut costs in their marketing budget, rather than trying to create a genuinely better experience for people who visit their website.

Ultimately, if you want to see incredible results from conversational marketing, you have to change your mindset and make a commitment to building a truly real-time conversational experience on your website.

Finally, one other way we see companies fail is by not using existing content they've produced to better and more thoroughly answer questions. To illustrate, let's say you've created an 80 percent video as an organization. If someone in a live chat asks you a question that is answered in that video, it's incredibly easy to send a link immediately to the visitor to allow that person to get a more thorough answer than you could possibly explain in a chat conversation.

Truly following the They Ask, You Answer philosophy naturally feeds your ability to give great answers to website visitors during chat experiences.

2. **If we decide to use live chat on our website, who should be responsible for responding to website visitors?** We hear this question a lot. That's because many of the businesses we talk to are worried that they either don't have enough people to staff any sort of live chat on their website or they'll put the wrong people in charge of responding to those live chats. Those concerns are completely understandable, but there is not really a wrong answer.

If you start small and experiment on one or two pages at first, a sales coordinator, marketing manager, office assistant, or receptionist should easily be able to take on this responsibility at first. It doesn't actually matter who that person is—all that matters is you're putting yourself out there and doing it.

For instance, even though HubSpot is a very large organization, they started out by assigning only a couple of people within the company some percentage of conversational marketing responsibilities. This allowed them to ensure that all customer-facing functions understood how to use conversational marketing successfully to make the customer experience better.

Or, using ourselves as an example, we have more than 60 people working at IMPACT. When we started out with real-time conversations, we only assigned one person to respond to live chats—a sales operations specialist. Now we have two people from our marketing team who take turns having conversations with website visitors during business hours, in addition to their other more primary responsibilities.

Once we moved beyond our initial experimentation phase and wanted to institutionalize real-time conversations for IMPACT more broadly and formally, those two individuals trained the rest of our marketing team on how to use our conversational tools, in the event additional support is required.

Again, how you decide to make those assignments is entirely up to you. If you start small, you'll give yourself the ability to be much more thoughtful and agile in how you scale up your conversational efforts.

3. **Due to [our industry, the length of our sales cycle, our average deal size, etc.], would conversational marketing even work for us? My gut says no.** For most businesses, it's very difficult to imagine real-time conversations simply because no one (or almost no one) is doing it in your space. But what happens when they are? What happens when real-time conversations become the norm? Sadly, most organizations are more worried about their competition than they are about what buyers really want. Let's not make that mistake.

Will real-time conversations ever be big in your space? Time will tell, but I certainly wouldn't bet against it.

4. **How would you prioritize conversational marketing against the other teachings and tactics found in They Ask, You Answer?** We teach our clients to focus first on answering their customers' questions through text and video on their website. If you do this well, you'll be able to offer a way better chat or conversational experience for your customers as well.

We don't suggest you try to do all of this at once. Essentially, follow the order of the book. Allow it to guide your priorities to eliminate overwhelm and ensure optimal results.

5. **We know what conversational marketing looks like now, but what will it look like in 10 years?** You know, that's a question I wanted an answer to myself, so I asked both Jon and Dave for their thoughts, since both of their organizations are well known for innovating and experimenting in the conversational space.

Jon shared that he could imagine a world where a business's homepage is simply a bot. In his vision of the future, "when you land on someone's homepage, your only option is to engage with a bot that will get you exactly where you want, as quickly as possible."

Dave, on the other hand, posited that the future of conversational marketing will be much less focused around specific tactics. Instead, in response to the increasing demand from consumers to have their expectations—whatever they may be—immediately met, he believes marketing will be much less about broadcasting one-way messaging and will look more like a "two-way communication channel."

As for me personally, I think the spirit of both of their answers is correct.

While I can't speculate precisely what conversational marketing will look like 10 years from now, I believe we will continue to see consumers demand more personalized, real-time experiences that feel more human and conversational. And those interactions will need to happen on their terms, whenever they feel they need help.

It's simply the next natural evolution of They Ask, You Answer.

52 | Self-Selection

The Next Phase of Search, Sales, and the Way We Buy

In the marketing section of this book, we discussed the way we've evolved as buyers and how we've learned to search online to find the answers we're looking for.

Since the first edition of this book came out, a very interesting buyer trend has continued to revolutionize not just this "search" process, but also the very sale itself.

Allow me to explain.

A recent Google study on trends is eye-opening.

Phrases searched (in Google) that include the words "for me" exploded by more than 120 percent in the last two years. In other words, when we first started using the internet, and we wanted to buy an in-ground swimming pool, we likely searched the phrase "in-ground swimming pool."

Then we evolved. We learned that *specificity* was the key.

Which is why we started searching phrases like "**best** in-ground swimming pool." But that is not where the evolution of search, or They Ask, You Answer, stops.

Hence the "for me" phenomenon.

Today, more and more, you're seeing that same swimming pool shopper search the phrase: "**best** in-ground swimming pool **for me**."

What does adding "for me" do exactly? Why are we adding it?

Once again, our expectations as consumers on digital and artificial intelligence are so high that we expect the internet (and businesses) to "know us"—and therefore identify exactly what we need for our specific situation.

Examples of extremely common "for me" searches are:

"What is the best car for me?"
"What is the best diet for me?"
"What is the best dog food for my dog?"

But "for me" isn't the only online search trend that shows how we're evolving. Searches that include the words "should I" and "do I need" have also both increased by more than 60 percent in the last two years.

"Sounds nice Marcus, but how do I apply this to my business? And what does it mean for making **They Ask, You Answer** *work in my situation?"*

To answer that, I'll share an experience that recently happened with my daughter, Danielle, as it encapsulates everything that this "for me" trend represents.

Wix: A Classic Case Study on Giving Buyers What They Want in Real-Time

A high school senior about to graduate, Danielle came to me and said, "Dad, I'd like to start a business while I'm in college. But currently, I don't have a website." I suggested she try Wix.com, a website-building platform that allows users who are not code- or tech-savvy to build their own websites.

Immediately, she popped open her laptop and, as I sat next to her on the couch, we visited the Wix.com website.

What happened next represents the future of how buyers think, and what's possible for businesses if they're truly willing to address what these buyers want. When you land on their website, Wix immediately points you toward a button that says, "Get Started." Seeing this, and ready to feel like she was making progress, Danielle quickly clicked it.

Next, the entire website interface changed.

Instead of bringing up a typical website page with navigation, buttons, and so on, we were faced with a clean white screen and a simple statement Danielle was meant to complete: *"I want to create a site for* _____*."*

The options were myself, a client, a company I work for, and someone else.

Notice the way this was phrased? Wix has used "first person" positioning for their messaging.

Why?

Because they wanted Danielle to feel a sense of specificity and ownership throughout the process. It was for her—her website, her business.

After she clicked "myself," another sentence appeared after the first one. It read: *"It should be a* _____*site."*

As she hovered over the blank, it gave her multiple options, at which point she chose "a beauty and wellness" site. She further clarified it was to be a website for a "makeup artist."

Next, Wix showed another question on the screen: *"What type of makeup artist would you like to be?"* After seeing multiple options to choose from, Danielle chose "makeup artist for weddings."

Before we continue, keep in mind this whole process—from the time she brought up the website to now—has taken less than two minutes.

The experience created by Wix is interactive, easy, and friction-free. But more than anything else, *Danielle* is in control. She is dictating, at least in her mind, the buying experience.

Next, Danielle was asked: *"Does your website need any of the following features?"*

After clicking "online bookings and appointments," what came next was arguably the most important question of the experience.

Wix said: *"What is your business name?"*

Upon seeing this, Danielle thought for a second, looked at me, and asked, *"Dad, what do you think? What's the right name?"*

You see, up to this point, Danielle's makeup business was just an idea. But now, with Wix asking her for a name, her idea had become real.

That's the beauty behind what Wix is doing with this interactive questionnaire. Each question builds on what came before it, adding more specificity to the type of business and making it feel even more personalized to the user.

After a few moments of quiet contemplation, Danielle smiled and typed in the name: *"Natural Beauty."*

Next, Wix showed Danielle some different designs and styles for a website and asked her which she preferred. Once she had selected her desired choice, Wix simply responded with: *"Now I'm going to create your homepage."*

Less than five minutes in, and Danielle is about to see the homepage of her website. And she hasn't yet spent a dime.

Was she excited? *Of course.* Was she enjoying the process? *Absolutely.*

Seconds later, Wix, based on all the questions Danielle had answered, showed the first rendering of her new homepage. There it was on the screen:

"Natural Beauty by Danielle"

She was all smiles. Then she looked at *me* and smiled. *"Dad, credit card!"*

Yep, Danielle, in her mind, already owned that website. It was now official.

Five minutes ago, she had an idea. Now she had a business name, a website, and clear excitement.

Well done, Wix. **Well done.**

I personally was mesmerized with this entire buying experience. But if you really understand the principles of They Ask, You Answer, it all makes sense.

In the digital age, buyers have certain expectations:

- They want it **fast**.
- They want it **personalized**.
- They want it to be **easy**.

And they want to be able to do as much of the buying experience as possible without anyone or anything deterring their efforts. This is the essence of self-selection and self-configuration, and it's only going to grow in importance for all businesses—B2B, B2C, service, product, etc.

How to Use Self-Selection Tools for Your Business

I hope that, by this point, you're considering how you could implement self-selection tools for your business. Let's take my swimming pool company as an example. Two of the most important and thoughtful questions customers have to answer are:

"What is the best type of in-ground swimming pool for me?"

"What is the best swimming pool shape and size for my yard?"

Much of the River Pools sales process is dedicated to helping someone answer those questions. That said, the majority of buyers, whether we like it or not, would rather know this before they talk to one of our sales team members.

For this reason we are in the process of developing interactive tools for the website that allow someone to answer a set of questions—the same ones our sales team would ask during an appointment—and receive a personalized answer recommending the right solution for their needs.

At IMPACT, we have created a similar tool, and its effect on our business has been astounding.

At impactbnd.com/scorecard, you can receive an immediate numerical score and assessment of how well your business is adhering to the principles of They Ask, You Answer, based on your input. Then you'll be given a personalized roadmap of the next steps you need to take to increase your company's adoption of a They Ask, You Answer culture.

If you're like many people I've spoken with about self-selection, you may be thinking the following: *"I see how this makes sense, Marcus, but aren't you afraid by doing this you'll diminish the sales team's role and hurt your ability to truly differentiation yourself from your competitors?"*

That's the beauty of They Ask, You Answer. Instead, in these moments, you should ask yourself, "But would I want this if I were the customer?"

That type of buyer-focused question should always be your compass. Of course, in this case, the answer is almost always "Yes!"

Since implementing this tool at IMPACT, leads have exploded on our website. Although we were doing well before, we have dozens of qualified companies taking the assessment daily, many of which turn into leads—leads that are much further along in the sales process.

That's self-selection sales tools at work.

They actually make your sales conversations way more effective because, in order for people to self-select, they naturally do more research, which in turn works them further down the sales funnel.

So think about the major questions your customers have to consider during the buying process. Could you create a tool that replicates or even enhances this process on the front end of the buying experience through your website?

You may be tempted to say, *"There's just no way we could do this unless it is face-to-face."*

But keep in mind that in the future the way we buy—fast, personalized, friction-free—isn't going to stop or slow down. It's always better that you, as a business, come up with the next way in which people make buying decisions, rather than waiting for your competitors to innovate first.

You don't want your competitors to rewrite the rules of doing business within your space, right?

Common Questions Regarding Self-Selection Tools

1. **What are the most common types of self-selection tools our business should consider?** The most common are *cost and pricing calculators*. More and more businesses allow users to at least get a "sense" for pricing, which is something we predicted in the first edition of this book and a trend that has only increased since that time.

Remember, pricing calculators don't have to provide exact numbers. But they should at least give potential buyers a feel for what they are getting into, financially speaking. Whether you sell a product or service, or are B2B or B2C, a pricing calculator is something you should strongly consider.

Another very common and impactful self-selection tool would be what we call a *design/build tool*. These are extremely important for many businesses and, once again, can be used just as well for designing a "service" as for a "product."

Here are some generic examples that could literally be used in almost any industry:

"Which plan is best for me?"
"What options should I go with?"
"How much _____ will I need?"

The third most common self-selection tool we've been involved with are *customer on-boarding tools*. In other words, once someone becomes a customer, we can create a self-selection tool that starts them off on the right foot working with us and keeps them on track. This type of tool can also help us identify and resolve any issues our new customer may be experiencing, which makes it extremely helpful for an internal customer service department.

2. **How much would it cost us to build one of these types of tools for our website?** The obvious answer to this question is "it depends." But because we've developed so many of these for our clients at IMPACT, I can tell you that the average price for something like this is in the $5,000 to $15,000 range, depending on the complexity of the application. That being said, there certainly are cases when the cost can be significantly higher.

3. **What are the biggest mistakes companies make when designing these types of experiences for their customers?** The biggest mistake companies make is assuming customers know what they are referring to when asking about options, features, tools, and so on. For example, in the case of a swimming pool, if the following were options on a pricing calculator, how many would you actually understand well enough to say "yes" or "no" to?

- Salt chlorine generator
- Tanning ledge
- Bottom drains
- Perimeter title
- 12-inch, 18-inch, or 24-inch cascade
- Elevated bond beam
- Inlaid tile
- Handrail
- Ozonator

As you can see, most people, even if they know what these are, wouldn't immediately be able to say, "I do (or do not) want that option on my swimming pool."

Therefore, the key to getting the most out of a self-selection tool is taking the approach that each question or item needs to be further explained. In other words, *assume ignorance.*

The simplest way to do this is by showing some type of "learn more" link next to the item, which points to an educational video or article. When you do this, you allow the customer to decide whether to perform a deep dive to further understand a particular feature.

4. **How can I see examples of self-selection tools in action?** Visit impactbnd.com/playbooks/selfconfig, where we have a continually updated collection of the best self-selection tools we've seen businesses use. Go there to be further inspired for ways you can create a better user experience for your customers going forward—ultimately increasing trust, transparency, and sales revenue in the process.

53

Website Priority 1

Proper Homepage Design and Messaging

Take a moment and think about what you consider important when visiting a company's website. Are you more concerned about you, your needs, and your questions—or are you more interested in hearing about the company you're visiting? Of course, the answer is we care more about ourselves—our priorities, our challenges, our questions.

Yet if you pay a visit to most business websites, what do most headlines immediately refer to? Them. Not you.

Why *they* are awesome.

What makes *them* unique.

Yes, those self-appointed superlatives and assertions do hold some value, but they should never be the focal point of a company's website messaging.

What are *your* buyers thinking the moment they land on your website? It comes down to this: *"Can (your company) solve my problem (need) or not?"*

That's it. That's what is on their minds.

Therefore, the headline of your homepage—as well as just about any other page on your site—should lead with your visitor's primary problems, needs, questions, or worries in *their* words. Only afterward can you begin to introduce your company, what value you can provide, how you can address their problems and/or answer their questions, and so on.

If you're curious how well your website messaging currently stacks up, here is an incredibly quick test you can use to assess the focus of your homepage copy, as well as the rest of the messaging on your website.

It's eye-opening: *Count how many sentences include the word "you" versus the number that include the word "we" or "our," as in "our company."*

The ideal ratio, from the customer's point of view, is 5 to 1 or better. In other words, you should refer to the customer five times more than you refer to you and your company.

I've seen many cases where the ratio was worse than 1 to 20. In other words, the business referred to themselves 20 times more than they referred to the customer.

Crazy but true.

Homepage Layout

Before you can evaluate or make any changes to your homepage, you and your team first need to understand (and agree on) what the fundamental purpose of a homepage is: *To get the visitor to page 2.*

"Wait, what's page 2?"

By "page 2," we mean your website visitors have taken a step beyond your homepage, thus beginning the process of finding what they are looking for. To explain why this matters, consider this—what do we learn about someone who spends 20 minutes on your homepage, but doesn't visit another page of your site?

Absolutely *nothing.*

For all we know, he may have landed on the homepage and immediately become bored. So he opened another window in his browser, only to forget to close out your website until later.

But when a visitor goes to your "pricing" page, your "learning center," or a "self-assessment" area, we start to see a contextualized picture of this individual; a legitimate customer experience has occurred, and your relationship with her has begun.

Knowing this, the rule of thumb you want to follow is simple: Your goal with your homepage shouldn't be to "teach" visitors everything you want them to know.

Your homepage is there to allow them to find exactly what *they* want as quickly as possible. This is exactly why, in a majority of cases, your homepage should never feature paragraph after paragraph of text. Approach it more like Google's homepage — one simple box — instead of Yahoo! — a simple box lost among a million news items.

You can apply this principle by answering a simple brainstorming question with your team: *"What are the top actions/questions/needs someone would have if he or she were coming to our website right now?"*

Once you've come up with a list, rank them in order of "most" important. From there, look at your list and ask: *"How does our existing design and layout reflect what the buyer would actually want?"*

The answer is often quite telling and, admittedly, sometimes frustrating.

That said, if you use this process to make improvements, your homepage layout will not only be designed to meet the needs of your buyers, but it will also lead to a dramatically higher "dwell time" on your website.

The leads and sales will follow.

54 | Website Priority 2

Obsess Over Honest Education

Because so much of They Ask, You Answer is based on this principle, we don't need to explore the subject further. But when it comes to the practical application of your obsession over honest education, how do you test yourself to see where you are and what needs to come next — that is, what content do you need to produce? To answer that question, bring your team together for the following exercise:

Brainstorm the top 25 questions you hear from prospects regarding your products and/or services. How many of the answers to those questions are easy to find — or even available at all — on your website right now, either in text or video format?

If you're struggling to come up with questions, think back to The Big 5 topic categories discussed earlier — cost and pricing, reviews, best in class, problems, and comparisons.

Once you complete this review, consider the list of gaps you identify between the questions your buyers are asking and what your website actually addresses. This is your prioritized roadmap for the content you need to create.

55

Website Priority 3

Premium Education

Although so much of the education we offer buyers is found in articles, videos, and so on, we still want to offer those who want it the "full course" of meat and potatoes—commonly referred to by marketers as "premium content."

Examples of common premium content offers include:

- Ebooks and whitepapers
- Buying guides and physical brochures
- Downloadable templates, checklists, and workbooks
- Webinars or on-demand videos

To measure how well you meet the needs of your buyers through your premium content, ask yourself:

"If someone wanted to learn as much as possible about each of our products and/ or services, have we created and published enough premium content offers for them to do so? If we have, are those offers easy for our website visitors to find?"

Again, the gaps you identify should be part of your plan of action.

56

Website Priority 4

An Equal Mix of Textual and Visual Content

By now, you've read the chapters on video in this book, so you possess an understanding of how critical creating video content—lots of it—will be to your success. This means, of course, that your website needs to prominently feature video content in addition to traditional text-based content.

So ask yourself: *"If someone wants to **visually** learn about any of our products and services, could they do that on our website right now?"*

Every major page of your website should have at least one video that is specific to its subject matter, whether that's a particular product or service, your pricing, or another topic.

Remember, the essence of They Ask, You Answer is adjusting to the way consumers think, act, learn, and buy. Therefore, with the rise of "visual learners" in our society today, we have no choice but to offer multiple ways to learn about our products and services. In short, if you're only providing answers and solutions on your website via the written word, you're poised to fall behind.

57

Website Priority 5

Self-Selection Tools

We spent an entire chapter discussing this critical trend, so now it is time to put it into action. But where do you start? Consider the following to find your answer:

"When a customer has to make a 'choice' of any of our products or services, is there an interactive tool on our website that guides them through this process?"

58

Website Priority 6

Social Proof

Our entire online buying culture is based on our ability, as consumers, to easily see what others are saying about the products and services we're interested in purchasing. This is why, in many ways, customer service has become one of your most important marketing tools.

How is this possible?

Because if your customer service is great, they (the customers) *may* leave a positive review.

But if your customer service is terrible, there is a high chance they'll leave a negative review.

In either case, other potential buyers will see those reviews and possibly make their buying decisions based on their impression of what someone else said about you. Thus, the intersection between marketing and customer service.

For this reason your organization should be prolific about social proof—what others are saying about you—on your website. Examples of social proof include customer journey videos, testimonials, client case studies, Net Promoter Scores (NPS), and so on.

If you are short on social proof, identify some of your happiest customers. Then ask them to record their journeys as buyers. Leverage these videos on your site and throughout your sales process.

59 | Website Priority 7

Site Speed

"Marcus, what does something technical like site speed have to do with content and everything else we've discussed in this book?"

Well, if you think about it, the speed of your website has everything to do with They Ask, You Answer, as well as the way we've evolved as buyers today. As buyers, we want it—answers, access, solutions, etc.—fast. And we want it **now**.

In fact, Google recently found that 40 percent of consumers will abandon a website page entirely if it takes more than three seconds to load.

Ouch.

If we consider that the average load time for most business websites is eight to 12 seconds—depending on factors like country, industry, etc.—you can imagine the astronomical number of visitors lost every single day by businesses with slow site speed.

What should you do? First, check out your site speed. Three great places to do this online, for free, are:

www.webpagetest.org
www.gtmetrix.com
www.thinkwithgoogle.com/feature/testmysite

If you test your site and notice a problem, talk with a technical SEO specialist and/or your webmaster and do whatever is necessary to speed things up. The negative impacts of slow speed—and, therefore, a slow user experience—are just too great a risk to ignore.

The bottom line of successful website design goes back to the core of They Ask, You Answer: *"Would I want this if I were the buyer?"*

As long as you look at these exercises from the perspective of your buyers, and not through the lens of your business, your website will easily stand out in a digital sea of mediocrity. Ultimately, this is the only way you'll produce the results you seek.

PART VI

Your Questions Answered

The title of this book, as you well know by this point, is *They Ask, You Answer.* I've discussed these principles with hundreds of organizations around the world, and I'm pretty certain you still have a few questions about them.

And nine-and-a-half times out of 10, I've heard them and answered them many times before. In this final part of the book, I address and answer the most frequently asked questions I've received from companies.

Simply put, it is my goal as the author to help you through what you've learned herein—assuming you're interested—to immediately commence your own content marketing efforts following the guidelines suggested in this book.

In order to do this, you are likely to need a few additional pointers on some of the detailed questions that most organizations ask as they're getting started.

60

"How Do I Find More Time to Make This Work Within My Organization?"

Far and away, one of the most common reasons companies say that haven't been able to achieve success with content marketing comes down to one variable: *time*. Individuals and companies are struggling—mightily—to find the time to produce content.

And I get that. It's not necessarily easy. It won't happen overnight. But, when done right, it's always worth it.

This being said, there are ways you can produce more content, at a faster rate, and more effectively. Some have been touched on already in this book. Others have not. Either way, they all work, as we've used them with our clients many times.

Create Blog Posts from Emails That Answer Questions Very Well

I'm amazed at just how much content (through email) the average business produces in a day. Many of these emails are to prospects and customers, answering their questions, giving them the information they seek. Sadly, most of this content is never used again. One might call it a "content marketing tragedy."

Here at IMPACT, we've seen client content production explode simply by adding one step to their educational (They Ask, You Answer) emails—bcc-ing someone in the marketing department to ensure that the content (assuming it's a fit) will be used in the future. By simply adding this click of a mouse, content ideas are continually being generated, the marketing team keeps its fingers on the pulse of all the questions and issues the sales team are dealing with, and silos are torn down.

It's powerful. **Do it.**

Start Talking to Yourself Out Loud. A Lot.

We live in the digital age. At this point, we can drive down the road, talk into our phone as if to a customer, and record everything we say. We can send that recording to a transcription company, who in turn quickly sends us a text-based copy, and voilà—a blog article has been written.

Considering most business owners are better talkers than writers, this is a powerful way of producing a lot of solid content, fast. Of course, this isn't the only way to do it; someone in the content department can easily do a sit-down interview with a thought leader, ask questions, and walk away with plenty of valuable content. Again, this is why having a content manager matters so much.

Participate in Blogathons or Videoathons with Employees

If you have employees and want to create a lot of content in a short period of time, a blogathon just might be the perfect solution. By getting everyone in the office away from writing emails and assigning articles and videos to work on—all together and at one time—a company can truly do amazing things.

In fact, we recently had a client in the financial space produce more than 50 pieces of content in one day—all because they set aside the time with their team to get it done without distraction.

Hire a Content Manager *Yesterday*

We mentioned this one in an earlier chapter, but it's simply too important not to re-emphasize. Someone must own the content marketing
efforts within the company, and that same person is key in involving
everyone else.

Remember That Insourcing Is a Very Big Deal

Remember, if someone is a subject matter expert of any type and spends
any time at all communicating with clients and customers, that person
could be producing content for your organization right now — all people
need is the platform and guidance to do so.

Learn How Each Employee Best Communicates and Run with It

Companies that produce great content understand that not everyone com-
municates the same way. Some prefer to write it out. Some prefer to talk it
out. Some would rather act it out on video.

Therefore, identify how your employees communicate and encourage
each individual to contribute to the process in the way he or she conveys
information best. Some people are great at researching, interviewing, and
writing; others are great at performing in front of a camera; and others may
not be great at either, but because of their knowledge make great interviewees.

In short, when you leverage the strengths of every team member, you
can dramatically reduce the time you spend in the production process and
get the most bang for your buck.

Turn on the Camera and Hit Record

Some of the greatest successes I had with my swimming pool company
occurred when my business partner Jason and I would walk onto a job site,
look around, and just start explaining everything we saw. In a few hours'

time, we had produced multiple videos, many of which today have hundreds of thousands of views on YouTube.

Keep in mind, most of these videos weren't planned out. We simply looked at the job, asked ourselves what the consumer might want to know about it, and then began talking.

This principle can be applied to any business, and, boy, does it save some serious time in the process.

Stop Doing the Thing That Does Not Bring the Greatest Returns

Every company has inefficiencies. This is certainly the case with marketing departments as well. Often we are doing marketing and advertising campaigns because we think we're "supposed to," not because there is a clear strategic purpose—one that has been proven to get powerful results.

If most companies had any idea just how much financial impact a smart content marketing campaign would have on their organizations, they would drop in a heartbeat much of what they are currently doing from a business development and marketing perspective.

Is It Really About Time, or Is Something Else Going on Here?

As humans, when we do not value something enough, we have a simple fallback response: "I don't have the time."

Granted, sometimes this statement is true.

But the majority of cases I've seen are cut and dried: the company's leadership team didn't "get it." They didn't truly understand content marketing and They Ask, You Answer. They didn't see its potential impact and were not emotionally invested.

When I was about to lose my company in 2009 and working well over 60 hours a week, I didn't have time to write articles and produce videos to put on our company website.

So I stopped watching TV.

I went from eight to six hours of sleep a night.

I looked for every extra second to create more content.

I did all of this because I didn't have a choice. I was looking over the cliff, simply trying to do anything I could do to hang on.

I'm not implying that you (the reader) fall into this category, but please ask yourself if it truly is about "time" or if something quite different is the issue.

61

"How Long Will It Take They Ask, You Answer to Work?"

"If we embrace content marketing as a company, and truly follow They Ask, You Answer as you're telling us, what does success look like? And how long would you expect this to take?"

This, quite possibly, is the top question companies have when they want to embrace this business philosophy. The question makes sense. Creating a culture of listening, teaching, and then acting on what you find isn't easy. It takes time, tools, resources, and major dedication.

It's also really worth it when done right.

Content Marketing the "Right" Way

As you might imagine, the following guideline can vary dramatically from company to company and industry to industry. Also, what you're reading here is contingent on doing content marketing the "right" way—as explained in this book.

287

Specifically, the following assumes that your company is:

- Producing at an absolute minimum two to three new pieces of content each week (videos, articles, and so on).
- Following the philosophies of They Ask, You Answer—a willingness to truly address the most common buying questions a prospect or customer is going to ask, about costs, problems, comparisons, reviews, and so on.
- The company is fully participating. From management to sales to marketing, everyone is involved, and a mission statement—stating the vision of They Ask, You Answer for your company—has been created.

5 Stages of Content Marketing Success

Assuming you're willing to do these three things, here is a realistic five-stage, three-year time frame and measuring stick of success:

- Hit "publish" and get the sales team engaged.
- Searchers and search engines realize you exist.
- Finally...you get leads.
- Generate sales and revenue.
- The snowball is rolling down the mountain.

1. Months 1–3: Hit "Publish," Get the Sales Team Engaged, and Implement Assignment Selling Immediately

Rarely do amazing things happen in content marketing without an incredibly consistent production and editorial calendar. For many companies, this is a major hurdle they've never been able to overcome.

But successful organizations have identified someone on staff who owns the content production process (content manager), their employees from other departments (sales, management, and others) are involved, and the content "machine" is starting to run nicely. Although the process won't happen overnight, it is realistic to expect it to happen within the first 30 to 90 days after launch.

Also, keep in mind the *immediate victories* that can, and should, occur within the first 90 days. For example, if you're producing The Big 5 content, then you're clearly addressing the top questions your sales team is receiving. This content should be integrated into the sales process as soon as it's produced. If you complete your 80 percent video, your sales team should integrate that into their sales communications immediately.

Remember, every piece of content produced should be viewed as another tool in the sales team's toolbox.

2. Months 2–5: Searchers and Search Engines Realize You Exist

The majority of business websites, at least before they embrace They Ask, You Answer, are relatively static (same old information, few changes). Because of this, they get little respect from searchers (consumers) and search engines alike. Furthermore, a new (or very young) website gets even less respect from search engines from a keyword ranking standpoint.

But once a company shows a true dedication to content production and is sticking with its editorial calendar, not only are viewers impressed, but search engines are as well.

What does this mean? Well, a few things.

Your website's SEO will improve (more keyword phrases will start to rank well), Google will index your site more often, and the speed at which your content starts to produce results will increase.

Sure, this usually doesn't happen until the 60- or 150-day mark, but when it does occur it's the first sign that traffic, leads, and sales are on the cusp of a continual increase for months to come.

However, a significant factor that dictates your ability to have search engines recognize your content is how saturated your niche or industry already is. In industries where everyone is producing content (like digital marketing companies), it's difficult to rank well in search engines. But among those industries that produce much less content, the lack of competition allows for quicker results.

Regardless of the amount of content saturation, though, your company should still strive to become the most trusted and transparent thought leaders of your space. Otherwise, great results are impossible to achieve.

3. Months 3–6: Finally, You Get Leads

Now that traffic is really starting to pick up, it's time for leads. Remember, the whole purpose of content marketing—aside from engaging prospects and customers and building trust—is to increase leads and ultimately generate sales.

Beyond the blog articles and videos, an effective content marketing campaign includes calls-to-action on the site, premium pieces of content (such as ebooks, buying guides, whitepapers, and so on), and other components.

Now that leads are starting to come in, it's critical to measure where they are coming from. Always look at your leads and the piece of content that brought them to the website. If that lead at some point becomes a customer, and you know his or her originating piece of content, you can track value back to that one single article, video, tweet, or other source.

As you might imagine, your ability to do this is critical for the long-term success and buy-in of your They Ask, You Answer efforts. It also shows you where you need to spend more or less of your time, resources, and attention.

4. Months 4–18: Generate Sales and Revenue

Finally, the day has come: you were able to track an actual sale back to your content marketing efforts. The importance of this transaction, and every one after this, is critical to the long-term success of the content marketing culture.

Depending on your company's sales cycles, along with a variety of other factors, the speed at which sales result from your content marketing efforts can vary tremendously. That being said, it should certainly happen before the first-year mark.

Furthermore, sales teams should be getting better and better at using the content that has been produced and injecting it throughout the prospect's sales experience.

5. Months 18–36: The Snowball Is Rolling Down the Mountain

For the first year or so, establishing an ultra-successful digital sales and marketing program can feel like you're rolling a snowball up a mountain. Frankly, it's no easy task.

But there does come a point, especially if you allow They Ask, You Answer to guide future strategy, that the snowball will reach the top of the mountain and start rolling down the other side, picking up momentum and growing bigger than your wildest expectations.

Many of the case studies you've read in this book, and the ones available at impactbnd.com/results, were certainly examples of this phenomenon. But it took time. It took people willing to own the program and management teams who made it clear to the team just how serious their content marketing efforts were.

Regardless of your industry or the size of your company, I truly believe these types of results are available for you. Of course, these numbers are just estimates. There are too many factors to list and too many variables in every company and industry to come up with hard numbers.

In spite of that, these parameters will, I hope, guide you along your content marketing journey and help you have a clearer vision of what to expect.

62 | "Are Content Marketing and They Ask, You Answer Just Fads?"

"Will content marketing even be around in 10 years once everyone has attempted to do it?" This question, and others like it, have been tossed my way at almost every presentation I've given on the subject over the past five years.

Unfortunately, for many of the folks asking the question, a lack of understanding about what content marketing is has led to inaction and a greater divide between them and their competitors—those who are willing to accept today's consumer and shift the way they market and sell accordingly.

What Is Content Marketing Exactly?

If we boil it down to its most basic characteristics, how would we define *content marketing* (assuming we weren't using "marketing speak") and They Ask, You Answer?

- Earning trust through teaching?
- Using great information to help others solve their problems?
- Listening to consumer questions and providing honest answers to those questions?

However you define it, these basic tenets have been around *forever*. Since the beginning of time, we've known that great communication, listening, teaching, and transparency all lead to trust. The same can be said in the future.

But today, because of the internet and the information age, we've given it a name: *content marketing*.

It's not a name I made up, and it's not one that many of our clients even use, as "They Ask, You Answer" (as a phrase) generally has a broader appeal across the organization. But either way, it certainly fits the bill to describe the process of using helpful and utilitarian information to earn trust with the digital consumer.

In the future, what will change about the way buyers develop trust with brands and ultimately make buying decisions?

- Will teaching still be relevant?
- Will helping others solve their problems still hold value and build trust?
- Will it be important to hear and address questions from your prospects and customers?

Yes, of course they all will be important.

Consumers will be vetting businesses like yours and mine more deeply than they ever have before. And when they stumble across a website (or whatever we call it in the future) that is truly a resource and a wealth of knowledge, they will stay.

So, is what we're talking about a fad?

Nope, it's a principle that has been around since the beginning and is not going anywhere anytime soon.

63

"How Can I Keep My Team Engaged in the Content Process?"

In order to overcome the engagement issue and help your team produce the type and amount of content they are capable of, it's critical to be creative. Simply saying, "Everyone, start blogging" will never be enough for developing a culture in which creating content is not simply something team members check off each month. There must be more.

Krista Kotrla of Block Imaging, whom we discussed earlier, has created a masterful culture of participation from dozens and dozens of employees in the effort to produce consistent, powerful company content.

The following list was inspired by some of the things Krista has done to keep the magic of They Ask, You Answer going at Block Imaging, plus some of the other creative ways clients have made They Ask, You Answer such a successful culture.

10 Ways to Keep Your Employees Motivated to Participate in Content Marketing

1. Focus Your Initial Content on the Bottom-of-the-Funnel Buyer Questions and Put It in the Hands of the Sales Team

Remember, quick wins are essential to great content marketing, and one of the mistakes many teams make is starting with questions that won't generate immediate results from a SEO or sales standpoint.

The Big 5 — cost, problems, comparisons, reviews, and best in class — are generally the most critical questions to tackle early on in the process. Once you have completed the answers, take these same pieces of content, stack them together in an organized way, and create ebooks, guides, video series, and so on, to enhance the sales team's capabilities to educate the prospect, earn trust, and close more deals.

2. Shine a Light on the Superhero Participants by Giving Them Awards and Team Recognition

Publicly tell the stories of why team members are being recognized so that others will learn from their example and, one hopes, want to copy them. Remember, if you can make the employees (especially those in the sales department) look like rock stars, others will naturally want to be a part of the "movement" as well.

3. Encourage the Team to Share Cross-Department Successes in Meetings

Create a segment for *others* to tell their success stories. It is really powerful when these experiences start popping up in other departments. An example of this would be a salesperson thanking an engineer for the blog article that was the catalyst for a lead contacting the company and ultimately turning into a customer.

4. Share Results and Celebrate Milestones

You can customize awards and recognition for your situation, but here are a few examples of milestones worth celebrating:

- Articles or videos that reach a thousand views
- Number of leads generated
- Views from organic traffic
- Ranking on page 1 of search results for target keyword phrases

Share recent deals and tie them back to the content that resulted in the customer experience. A great way to do this is to create a quarterly newsletter that everyone on the team can read and see all of the highlights from that time period.

5. Create Some Team Goals to Strive Toward Together

Here are examples of activities you could consider:

- *Individual:* Five blog articles = slippers (something visible that they can wear around the office like a status symbol)
- *Collective:* 200 blogs = whirly ball (everyone gets to play)
- *Department versus department competition* (service team versus product team)
- *Individual versus individual face-off*

6. Make They Ask, You Answer Training Part of the Hiring and On-Boarding Process in Every Department

This should go without saying, but it's critical. Also, if you have an initial all-hands-on-deck workshop to kick off your inbound and content marketing efforts, make sure you video record it for future employees.

7. *Make It Easy for the Team to Share Content*

Want your employees to share content? Make it easy for them. Teach them how to do it. For example, you could introduce them to:

- *Lazy links:* A hyperlink to a website typed in by an instant messenger chat member while chatting because he or she is too lazy to open a browser, type in the URL, and click "enter."
- *Email signatures:* One of the simplest ways to point someone's attention to content, especially with all new signature tools available on the market today.
- *Social media:* Many more employees would share company content if they understood how to share it, when to share it, and why to share it. A little training can go a long way.

8. *Ask for Help in Very Specific Ways*

Remember, everyone wants to feel important, which is why "special tasks" or "missions" can be a great content marketing initiative. Here are a few examples:

> *"Hey, here's a strategic phrase that we don't rank for yet and it is an area you know a lot about. Could you address this topic so that people will find us when searching for an answer?"*
>
> *"Hey, Manager, we're not seeing any content from your department lately. Could you bring this up in your next team meeting to drum up some activity and participation? Your department is full of knowledge, and we need to get that knowledge out to the rest of the world."*
>
> *"We're going to take all of your greatest blog articles and start filming video versions as well. We want people not just to hear you, but see you as well. Here is a meeting invite for your first filming session."*

9. *Humanize It*

Always remind everyone of the real human beings that your content affects. How does it change lives? What is the deeper "Why?" to what they're being asked to do?

10. Stay Curious

Great digital sales and marketing leaders are always looking for an edge. Part of this is never being satisfied with being average and doing whatever it takes to become a world-class organization of teachers and listeners.

A big part of the process is knowing how to ask the right questions of your team.

Here are a few examples:

> *"You're really awesome at generating content on a regular basis. What is your secret to making it look easy? How have you worked it into your everyday life?"*
>
> *"Hey, thought you'd be interested to learn that 80 percent of your team members are contributing content. I'm curious to hear how I can make it easier for you to participate so that people can learn from you, too."*
>
> *"How can I make this easier for the team to participate? How can I make it more fun?"*
>
> *"How can I prove this is working?"*

The bottom line is this, folks:

It's about results.

This is exactly why you must get results, then tell the results, then celebrate the results, and, of course, improve results. *And*, while doing this, tell the stories that help everyone remember that this about *real people*.

Sometimes you have to lead by example. Sometimes you have to get in the trenches and work side by side. You have to empower others to equip and encourage one another. You have to set up a lot of feedback loops. You have to love the challenge of it. You have to build it into your culture.

No, it's not easy, but it is certainly worth it.

64

"I've Been Told If We're Not Adding Anything New to the Conversation, Then We Shouldn't Be Talking About It—Is That Right?"

One of the biggest fallacies I've heard come out of the mouths of "experts" in the digital marketing space is the concept that if someone (individual, company, or other entity) has already said (written about, talked about, produced a video about) something, then it's a waste of time for someone else to add their two cents—especially if they're not adding anything "new" to the conversation.

For lack of a better way of putting this: the people who make these statements are ignorant of the history of the world and completely missing the mark. You see, at this point (in the 21st century), most of what we say is a repeat of what someone else has already said.

In this book, I've espoused honesty, transparency, and great teaching to gain trust in business. Is this a new concept? No, it's older than dirt. But I'm explaining it my way, with my stories, in my language.

And because I'm willing to take the time to explain it here, two parties benefit.

For many readers, this may be the book that finally touches them in such a way that they take action by becoming obsessive listeners, problem solvers, and teachers in their space—something that will generate more trust and ultimately new business. This increase in business will lead to increased revenues, enable them to hire more employees, and ideally to live a life of financial peace.

You might read those words and think I'm exaggerating, but I'm not. I've seen the results again and again. I've been talking about the importance of They Ask, You Answer for almost a decade. I've been blogging about it, producing videos about it, and speaking on stages around the world about it.

I've seen what can happen when individuals, businesses, and brands embrace this philosophy, many of whom have contacted me after the fact and told me touching stories of the impact of the change—personally and professionally.

This brings me to the other party that benefits: *me.*

By writing this book, I'm being forced to take everything I've learned and distill it into words. I've been challenged to research deeper, think harder, and articulate my thoughts and experiences more clearly. And because of this, I will finish this book a better communicator on this subject than I was when I started.

You see, by producing content, regardless of how many times "it has been said," we become better people, better employees, better sales professionals, and better communicators.

That's how it works. And that's how it has worked for thousands of years.

Before I finish my thoughts on this subject, just look at the most popular book of all time: The Bible. Anyone who has read the Books of Matthew, Mark, Luke, and John of the New Testament know these Gospels are very similar. In fact, there is quite a bit of redundancy across the four books.

But what would have happened if Luke had said, *"Well, Matthew already talked about this, so I think it would be a waste of time for me to talk about it as well."* History would have changed entirely.

Regardless of your thoughts on the Gospels, I hope you see my point here.

This is why I truly believe every individual and every company needs to write what I call "The Gospel According to *You*."

- Your prospects and customers want to know your thoughts and feelings.
- They want to know what you believe and why you believe it.
- But *you* also need to experience this.
- You need to distill your thoughts.
- You need to state your company's doctrine.

By so doing, you'll positively affect every party involved. You'll become better teachers and communicators. You'll be more in touch with what your customers are thinking. And you'll gain their trust.

65

"Can I Just Hire an Agency to Do This for Me?"

I've been asked many, many times by audience members and readers whether they can simply hire an agency to do all of this content and digital "stuff" suggested in *They Ask, You Answer*. Truthfully, I could take the easy route and tell you, "Yes, of course, an agency could do this for you just as well as you could do it yourself." Heck, I own an agency. We do this stuff for clients.

But the fact is that if I said that, I'd be lying.

The world of inbound and content marketing has proven this time and time again. Case in point, my agency, IMPACT, provided traditional inbound marketing services to clients like every other agency in the space for years.

And the results? Incredibly *average*.

Sure, we were able to build nice websites, help clients rank for some new keywords, and build better marketing campaigns. But it wasn't until we decided to offer a consulting model—where we *taught* other companies the "how" of inbound, content, and They Ask, You Answer—that we started to see world-class case studies and to empower our clients to shoot to the top of their industries.

In all fairness, having an agency do this for you is way easier than learning to do this yourself in-house.

You don't have to learn a new culture.

You don't have to involve your sales team.

You don't have to embrace a radically transparent way of doing business.

You don't have to hire people in-house to "own" the work for you.

All you have to do is pay your retainer each month, and you'll get a performance report of your results from your marketing agency.

Still, there is another option. A better option.

As I like to say, **you** can hold the paintbrush.

You can create the art.

You can develop the culture where silos are eliminated and everyone—sales, marketing, and leadership—"gets it."

You can play by your own rules and produce as much great content as you want, without the limitations of a retainer to hold you back.

Sure, you may need some guidance at first. But, in the long run, you will be the artist, learning to create your own masterpiece. And that, I believe, is what every business should be striving for.

Today, our philosophy at IMPACT is the very one that revolutionized my swimming pool company and continues to achieve amazing results for businesses around the world.

Give a man a fish, you'll feed him for a day.

But teach him *how* to fish, you'll feed him for a lifetime.

That may be the greatest result of They Ask, You Answer, and all the stories I've heard from readers around the world. Literally hundreds and hundreds of businesses, embracing this sense of ownership, seeing themselves as teachers, and becoming the voice of trust within their space.

It's not going to be easy.

But if (and when) you do pull it off, it **will** be worth it.

66

"How Can We Afford to Do This?"

So, here we are, closing out the book.

If you're like many of the company leaders I speak with—regardless of how big or small your business is—you very well may be saying to yourself at this point: *"You're asking a lot, Marcus. **How can we afford to do this?**"*

Here's the funny thing about this question. If you take companies like Yale Appliance, Mazzella, or others that have won big with They Ask, You Answer, the *last thing* on their minds once they've started experiencing success with They Ask, You Answer is "How can we afford this?"

Rather, they're thinking:

*"Should we hire **more** people?"*
*"Should we hire **another** videographer?"*
*"Should we hire a **second** writer/content manager?"*

We've suggested you take on three major expenses:

- The cost of a full-time content manager
- The cost of a full-time videographer
- The cost of a tool that fully measures the ROI of all your digital sales and marketing efforts

*Combined, the sum of these three expenses is equivalent to hiring **a single salesperson** for most companies.*

Think about that.

Could a single salesperson have made the financial impact that Yale Appliance, Mazzella, Block Imaging, and others achieved by following the principles of They Ask, You Answer?

Not in a million years.

That's the beauty of They Ask, You Answer. It allows you to have a financial impact on your business at such an incredible scale simply by adding a few positions that most companies still, to this day, refuse to add because they wrongfully consider those investments to be a "marketing expense" instead of a "sales driver."

But let's not stop there.

Do you think this is going away?

That these trends will slow down or reverse themselves?

Since *They Ask, You Answer* was published in early 2017, the strategy has only grown in importance. Those who have embraced it as a culture are now light years ahead of others in the marketplace. Many of those companies that have not are now, sadly, falling behind. I meet those leaders in my audiences every day, and sometimes their stories are truly gut-wrenching.

That's what's so scary and, at the same time, exciting about the digital transformation we're all experiencing in the world of business right now.

Digital is the great equalizer.

Those willing to shift their mindset and do the work can make a quantum leap in their industry and bypass their largest competitors. Those that refuse to listen to buyers and the way they've changed are experiencing tremendous frustration and potential financial ruin.

So don't ask, "Can we afford to do this?" Instead, I challenge you to answer these hard questions:

"What if we don't do anything?"
"What is the cost on inaction?"
*"Can we afford **not** to do this?"*

67

A Revolutionary Marketing Strategy

As I look back on the past decade, it almost seems like a dream. One day, I'm a pool guy on the brink of losing my business. The bank is calling. My credit cards are maxed out. My employees are sitting home. As a father and husband, I'm failing.

And then, what seems like the next day I'm traveling the world and helping businesses become their best selves while speaking to audiences of hundreds or thousands of people. It's amazing. Really amazing. More important, as a father and husband, I'm present. Believe it or not, I'm home way more now than I ever was as a struggling pool guy.

Simply put, we are happy. We are blessed.

The River Pools and Spas story became very well known in the digital space when I experienced a very fortunate event in 2013. That year, I was speaking at a conference in Dallas, Texas. After my talk, a reporter came up to me and said he would like to do a story on how we were able to save River Pools through such a simple strategy as listening, teaching, and transparency.

Frankly, I didn't think much of this reporter's request until we spoke on the phone for 90 minutes a few days later. A few days after that, he sent a photographer to my swimming pool company.

What happened next is when my life changed very much.

Four days after the photographer showed up at River Pools and Spas, the following article (see Figure 67.1) appeared on the cover of the small business section of the *New York Times*:

Figure 67.1　River Pool and Spas Featured in the *New York Times*.

If you look at the article, you'll notice a peculiar irony. Notice the title? *"A **Revolutionary** Marketing Strategy: Answer Customers' Question."*

Folks, is there really anything "revolutionary" about answering your customer's questions? In principle, no. But in practice? Yes, absolutely.

This became the number 1 shared and emailed story for the small business section of the *Times* during the next three days. They even re-ran the article as a blog post on Saturday that same week.

Without question, the story resonated.

I was shocked to find that it resonated so much that over the coming months I received more than 1,000 emails from business owners and marketers all over the world. Almost all of these emails said one of two things.

The first comment everyone wanted to make was: *"Marcus, that thing you did with your pool company is so simple. I just can't believe how simple it is!"*

Yes, it was simple. But simple is good. This way, anyone, including you, can apply what we did at River Pools and Spas to your business. You just have to care enough about the customer to obsessively listen, teach, solve problems, and be honest in the process.

The second comment I received really often from people who had read the article sounded like this: *"Marcus, I feel like you've now given me permission to do that which I've always felt we should be doing."*

This one, to me, is the crux of the whole thing.

Throughout this book, if you've made it to this point, there probably have been many times where you've thought to yourself: *"I've been feeling like we should be doing this for a long time."*

So now, as we come to a close, I ask you to follow the instincts you already have. After all, we have them for a reason.

Be the best teacher in the world.
Obsess over their questions.
Answer with fierce honesty.
And win their trust.

End of Book Resources

Tools to Help You Embark on Your Own They Ask, You Answer Journey

Get Your Scorecard

Grade Yourself on They Ask, You Answer Right Now

If you've reached this far in the book, you're probably excited about the potential impact They Ask, You Answer will have on your business. But you are also asking yourself the following:

"Where is our organization right now with respect to doing They Ask, You Answer the right way?"

"What must we do first to start?"

It is for this exact reason my team at IMPACT has created an interactive tool—the They Ask, You Answer scorecard—that will help you find immediate answers to these two very important questions.

It consists of a series of questions that represent the most important teachings and principles of They Ask, You Answer, as well as the most successful content marketing and They Ask, You Answer case studies our organization has seen to-date.

By taking a few minutes to fill out the scorecard, you will be forced to truly reflect on where you are as a company, and then add clarity to the proper action steps to take next. It's not just an assessment—it's an investment in your future.

As you continue this journey, we invite you to keep coming back, so you can watch your score flourish alongside the corresponding impact They Ask, You Answer is having on your organization.

Get your They Ask, You Answer scorecard today at:
impactbnd.com/scorecard.

315

More They Ask,
You Answer
Resources

Congratulations! You now have the insights and know-how you need to create a true, lasting They Ask, You Answer culture at your company...but this is only the beginning of your journey. So what comes next?

To help you keep the learning and your momentum going—and to help you see the most success with the philosophies of the book, *They Ask, You Answer*—we've created the following resources for you...

They Ask, You Answer Scorecard

How well is your company embracing the principles of They Ask, You Answer? This personalized scorecard will tell you where you are right now and what exact next steps you should be taking.

impactbnd.com/scorecard

Real-World Results

Want to learn more about how other companies like yours achieved success with They Ask, You Answer? Watch dozens of companies share the stories of their unique journeys with They Ask, You Answer in these videos.

impactbnd.com/results

They Ask, You Answer Playbooks

You're ready to put They Ask, You Answer into action. But where do you start? What specific steps do you need to take? Learn everything you need to know from our extended They Ask, You Answer playbooks.

impactbnd.com/playbooks

Recommended Digital Sales and Marketing Software and Tools

Many of our favorite tools are free or come with a free trial.

impactbnd.com/tools

Free Templates and Downloads

Here you'll find many of the same tools we use with our clients at IMPACT.

impactbnd.com/downloads

Recommended Books and Further Reading

Go beyond *They Ask, You Answer.*

impactbnd.com/books

Finally, you can email me your questions, thoughts, or feedback at any time at marcus@marcussheridan.com. And if you'd like to learn more about having me speak at an event or facilitating a workshop for you, please visit marcussheridan.com.

Accelerate Your They Ask, You Answer Success with IMPACT

It's our obsession to help you best implement the principles you've read in *They Ask, You Answer* and achieve breakthrough digital sales and marketing success.

Consulting

Help your people get to the next level fast with content, HubSpot, and video consulting. **Learn more at impactbnd.com/consulting.**

Workshops

Get your entire company aligned with an IMPACT facilitated They Ask, You Answer workshop. Then, expedite your team's video game with IMPACT's two-day video workshop. **Learn more at impactbnd.com /workshops.**

IMPACT Live

Join more than 1,000 of the top digital sales and marketing leaders who practice They Ask, You Answer for IMPACT's annual event, IMPACT Live, in Hartford, Connecticut. **Learn more at impactbnd.com/live.**

IMPACT Elite

The Facebook group for They Ask, You Answer practitioners—free for all. **Learn more at impactbnd.com/elite.**

Acknowledgments

To my dear wife, Nikki, and my four kids—Danielle, JT, Larsen, and Pink—thank you for joining me on this amazing journey. You are my everything.

Although I'm unable to mention everyone that has had a hand in this book, I want to also thank:

Jim Spiess and Jason Hughes, my dearest friends and business partners at River Pools and Spas.

My incredible team at IMPACT and my business partner, Bob Ruffolo, for taking the ideas from *They Ask, You Answer* to another level. (We're just getting started, gang.)

My original band of brothers at The Sales Lion—it was a great ride.

Liz Murphy for contributing so much to this revised edition and treating it like her own book. She makes me look much smarter than I am.

Zach Basner for making video a culture within so many organizations and bringing that knowledge to this book.

Kevin Phillips for being the ultimate team player and contributing so much to the case studies found herein.

Jaime Rowland for helping me in so many ways, onstage and off.

And finally, to the teacher within each one of us—*this book is for you.*

About the Author

Marcus Sheridan is a highly sought-after international keynote speaker known for his unique ability to excite, engage, and motivate live audiences with his simple, yet powerful transformational business approach.

Marcus has been dubbed a "Web Marketing Guru" by the *New York Times* and in 2017 *Forbes* named Marcus one of 20 "Speakers You Don't Want to Miss." Not one to be limited to the stage, Marcus is most often found walking through the crowd, calling audience members by name, and bringing them into his presentation.

As author of *They Ask, You Answer*, Marcus has not only inspired thousands to achieve their potential, but has given them the tools they need to get there. Mashable rated his book the "#1 Marketing Book" to read in 2017. *Forbes* listed it as one of "11 Marketing Books Every CMO Should Read."

Marcus has been featured in the *New York Times, The Globe and Mail,* Content Marketing Institute, Social Media Examiner, and more. Marcus has spoken to companies such as Discover Card, Microsoft, eBay, McKesson, Cision, Whirlpool, Moe's, Genpact, Love Funding Group, and more. He has inspired thousands of audiences and helped millions of people from all over the world to achieve their own success with his They Ask, You Answer philosophy.

But Marcus's story didn't begin on the stage. It started with a business being created and run out of the back of a beat-up pickup truck. Marcus's experience of saving his swimming pool company, River Pools and Spas, from the economic collapse of 2008 has been featured in multiple books, publications, and university case studies around the world. From its humble beginnings as a three-man company, to one of the largest manufacturers and installers in the country, River Pool and Spas has the most visited pool website in the world, with over 750,000 hits a month.

Marcus's experience as an entrepreneur and business owner who had successfully saved his company led him to opportunities to share his story and help others. What started as speaking from the stage quickly turned into a sales and marketing consulting agency, The Sales Lion. Using his marketing principles, Marcus and his team led clients step-by-step through the process of growing and even transforming their companies.

In early 2018, The Sales Lion merged with IMPACT, establishing one of the most successful digital sales and marketing agencies in the country. Within his speaking company, Marcus Sheridan International, Inc., Marcus gives over 70 global keynotes annually during which he inspires audiences in the areas of sales, marketing, leadership, and communication.

Index

Note: Page references in *italics* refer to figures.

325

Disarmament principle
  Versus and/or Comparisons and,
    78–80
  in assignment selling, 140–141
Drift, 247

E

Editorial guidelines, 162–163
80 percent video process, 187–193
Email
  bio videos for email signatures, 195–197
  email signatures, 298
  follow-up, 135–137
  personalized video for, 215–219
  subject lines for, 217
  as teaching opportunity, 141
  text vs. video in, 218–219
  thumbnail of video for, 217–218
Everybody Writes (Handley), 97
Expertise. See Thought leaders

G

Gerdhardt, Dave, 247–248, 254
Goal orientation, of content managers, 170
Goals, setting, 297
Google
  homepage of, 265
  on website speed, 277
  See also Search engine optimization
    (SEO)
"Gospel According to You, The," 303
GoVideo (Vidyard), 216

H

Halligan, Brian, 174–175
Handley, Ann, 97
Health Catalyst (case study), 143–148
Horstmeier, Paul, 144–148
HubSpot
  conversational marketing by, 245, 248,
    250, 253, 254
  terminology used by, 18, 174–178
  website analytics and, 118
Hughes, Jason, 4–5, 61, 283

I

IMPACT
  "CarMax Effect" of, 34
  inception of, 14
  messaging by, 114
  video used by, 222 (*See also* Video
    production)
  work of, 47
  See also Assignment selling; Websites
Implementation
  Block Imaging (case study), 155–158,
    295
  content managers and, 56, 165–172
  insourcing and using your team for
    content creation, 151–153
  overview, 149–150
  power of insourcing for, 151–153
  tools for, 173–178
  workshops for, 159–163
Inbound and Content Marketing Made Easy
    (Sheridan), 67
Inbound marketing
  advertising vs., 99–100
  defined, 19, 23
  See also Big 5 content subjects; Content
    marketing
Influencers. *See* Triangle of Influence
In Planet, 94
Insourcing
  Block Imaging (case study), 155–158,
    295
  "Don't Stop" rule of, 218, 230–231
  in-house video culture and, 179–180,
    183, 229–234 (*See also* Video
    production)
  power of, 151–153
  for They Ask, You Answer, 283, 305–306
Internet
  for research, 17–19, 39–42
  video traffic on, 181–183
Interviewing
  by content managers, 169
  of videographer candidates, 225–227

J

Journalists, as content managers, 171